Conversation WITH God

Lloyd John OGILVIE

HARVEST HOUSE PUBLISHERS

EUGENE, OREGON

Cover photo © Photos.com

Cover by Koechel Peterson & Associates, Minneapolis, Minnesota

CONVERSATION WITH GOD
Formerly *Quiet Moments in Prayer*
Copyright © 1993 by Harvest House Publishers
Eugene, Oregon 97402
www.harvesthousepublishers.com

ISBN-13: 978-0-7369-2045-2
ISBN-10: 0-7369-2045-5

Library of Congress Cataloging-in-Publication Data

Ogilvie, Lloyd John.
  [How to have a conversation with God]
  Conversation with God / Lloyd John Ogilvie.
    p. cm.
  Originally published: How to have a conversation with God. c1993.
  ISBN 978-0-7369-2045-2 (pbk.)
  1. Prayer—Christianity. I. Title.
  BV215.O36 2007
  248.3'2—dc22

                                                          2007002950

Printed in the United States of America

07 08 09 10 11 12 13 14 15 / LB-SK / 12 11 10 9 8 7 6 5 4 3 2 1

✦

To Inez Smith

*In gratitude for our friendship
through the years*

✦

Contents

Part One

Learning the Art of Conversation

Intimate Prayer Is Conversation with God

Nothing is more important. It's the source of life's greatest joy. There's no power or peace without it. With it, we receive supernatural insight and wisdom. Our ability to understand and love people is maximized. We think more clearly and can act more decisively. Our problems shrink and we can tackle opportunities with gusto. Most of all, we fulfill the reason we were born: to know and love God.

I'm talking about the time we spend alone with God in prayer. Don't groan inside. This is not another "ought to" book about prayer to add to the guilt you may feel about the infrequency or shortness of your prayers. Rather, this is a "how to" book about a different way of praying.

Think of a time when you had a really satisfying conversation with someone who truly loves and affirms you. Remember how you felt? Respected, cherished, accepted. And because you felt love and admiration for this person, you sensed that it was safe to share your innermost thoughts and feelings. You wanted to listen to his or her thoughts. Give-and-take in the conversation flowed. You knew it was okay to laugh at yourself and were not embarrassed by your tears over your failures. After the conversation you felt refreshed, renewed by the delight of having someone be real with you and with whom you could let down your guard and be yourself.

Conversations like that are all too rare. Many husbands and wives have neither the time nor the sensitivity to have them. Friends seldom open up with each other. Fellowship with other Christians is no guarantee of deep, personal exchange.

There is only one Person with whom profound conversation is possible on a consistent basis. My use of the capital "P" has already told you who I think it is. God.

True Prayer Is Conversation with God

The use of the word *conversation* to describe prayer with the Creator, Redeemer, and Lord of all may have a presumptuous ring for some. For others it may seem too pedestrian. But for most of us, the question is whether a conversation with Almighty God is even a possibility.

We're much more experienced at monologue prayer. We praise God, thank Him for His blessings, tell Him about our concerns for people and the world conditions, ask for guidance, and commit the day to Him. It's like a one-way telephone conversation in which a person goes on endlessly without the slightest pause for even an "aha" from the other party and then hangs up before a response can be made.

Many of us have been conditioned to think of prayer as monologue because of public prayer in church. Often the pastoral prayer sounds like a newscaster summarizing the world news as if God didn't know! And in some of the prayers of friends we consider to be supersaints, they hardly take a breath between their magnificently worded phrases. So it's very understandable that conversation would be a strange way to think about prayer.

Years ago, I made getting to know God the primary commitment of my life. I tried to learn how to pray. At the beginning of each day I would have a quiet time in which I read a portion of the Bible and then gave my monologue prayer. At the end of my prayer, I would sometimes take time for silence. That time became increasingly shorter as greater demands were made on my life, and the pull of the day's challenges distracted me. I hate to admit it, but on most days I hung up on God before I had listened long enough to receive His wisdom and guidance.

One day I stumbled on a secular book about effective conversation. It described how to be a good listener as well as a talker in conversations. I learned that nothing destroys conversation more than long discourses that leave no room for response.

Then it hit me. What would it be like to have a conversation with God? I began experimenting. My pilgrimage in seeking to know God took a sharp turn.

First I learned that God begins the conversation. He calls us into dialogue with Him. The ordered steps of prayer flow naturally. We will talk about these steps of preparation, praise, confession, thanksgiving, meditation, intercession, supplication, guidance, and empowering in the chapters of this book. But the crucial thing I want to stress at this point is the importance of pausing to listen for the Lord's response between the steps of prayer.

The Bible is essential to the deeper quality of conversation with God. The Scriptures were inspired by the Holy Spirit not only as the infallible guide for faith and practice, but as the source of verses through which God guides us in each phase of prayer.

Magnificent promises are found throughout the Bible. These promises are direct quotes of God's words in the Old Testament and of Christ in the New Testament. They call us to prayer and lead us on from step to step in an evolving conversation of prayer. When we listen to the Lord in these promises and meditate on them, they instigate further thought and fresh inspiration in our minds. God does not contradict His promises in the Bible. He will be to us what He has said He will be.

The Scriptures also provide us with the language of response. They help us love God, to trust Him with our needs, and open ourselves to His guidance. More than just thought starters, they liberate our own words to express the longings of our hearts. The psalmists, wisdom writers, prophets, apostles, and other characters of the Bible teach us how to converse with God. Their words give wings to our own. They vibrate with life when we reword them in the first-person singular and pray them as our own prayers.

Then, as we pause to listen between each part of prayer, God speaks in both the Scriptures and in the thoughts He forms in our minds.

When the promises of God and the responses of inspired writers of the Scriptures are carefully arranged, they give us progression and power in our prayers. There are at least nine crucial steps of prayer outlined in the Bible based on clear admonitions about what we are to seek from God in prayer.

The chapters of this book are arranged to move through a conversation with God. We will discover biblical promises and responses for each step of the conversation. I have used these verses for years and they have not only deepened my understanding of what God wants and offers, but also of what I can dare to ask.

At the conclusion of the book I have provided thirty guides for using Scriptures in conversational prayer. My hope is that you will experience an exciting month of putting into practice what we have discovered about the steps of prayer. These daily guides can be repeated throughout the subsequent months of the year.

Before long you will memorize these verses of prayer and they will be in your mind and heart wherever you are. They will guide your prayers in the morning hours, through the day, before going to sleep, and when you are awakened during the night with worry or concerns.

Are you eager to learn how to have powerful conversations with God? The request of the disciples, "Lord, teach us to pray," expresses the longing of our hearts today. A daily time alone with God in conversation, listening to Him and responding, can change prayer from a duty to a delight!

2

God Begins the Conversation

A Highland Scots friend of mine has a colorful way of praying. I like the straightforward way he talks to God, but one day I became concerned about how he opened his prayer. "Dear God, I hope Ye're listenin', because I need Ye and I dinna ken whether Ye're in a good mood or not, but if Ye are, I've got some big problems that'll need Yer help."

As much as I appreciated my friend's vernacular veracity, I was disturbed by the underlying assumption of his prayer. Later, with the frankness we enjoy in our friendship, I said, "Something disturbs me about the way you began your prayer. You sounded like talking to God was your idea and that you had to get His attention."

He seemed open to what I was saying, so I went on: "Prayer is a conversation with God. He begins the conversation. The desire to pray is the result of His greater desire to have a deep communication of love with us. When we feel the need to pray it's because He's been at work in us. We don't need to get His attention—He wants our attention! Prayer starts with God."

"That's sure a different way o' thinkin' aboot prayer!" my friend exclaimed.

Indeed it is. And it's where we must begin our investigation of prayer as conversation. The first step of prayer is preparation: God's preparation of us. Long before we talk to God, He talks to us. He calls us into conversation.

Gently, but persistently, the Holy Spirit stirs our spirit. He creates a hunger and thirst for God. A sense of loneliness for God is a gift produced by the Spirit.

This changes the false idea that we have to search for God. He is in search of us. Pascal expressed this truth vividly: "I would not be searching for Thee, hadst Thou not already found me."

Listen to how God opens the conversation:

> It shall come to pass that before they call, I will answer; and while they are still speaking, I will hear (Isaiah 65:24).

This is my favorite verse to repeat when I feel the first stirring in my soul creating a desire to pray. Often it's what I hear God say when I begin my time alone with Him in the morning. These words prompt me to say, "Good morning, Lord. Thanks for beginning the conversation!"

Long before we think of praying, God is thinking of us. And this is what He goes on to say,

> For I know the thoughts that I think toward you, says the LORD, thoughts of peace and not of evil, to give you a future and a hope. Then you will call upon Me and go and pray to Me, and I will listen to you. And you will seek Me and find Me, when you search for Me with all your heart. I will be found by you, says the LORD (Jeremiah 29:11-14).

Talk about a conversation opener! Imagine someone you love and admire, and whose thoughts and opinions you cherish, saying to you, "You are constantly on my mind. And when I think of you they are wonderful thoughts of peace and future happiness for you. I'm pulling for the very best for you. What a joy it is to be your cheerleader!" It would not be difficult to find time for conversation with a person like that.

Multiply the best of human care and concern for us a billion times and you've only begun to fathom God's love for us as He calls us into conversation. That's the whole point of time alone with God. It is to allow Him the opportunity to love us.

He also wants to guide our thoughts and give us wisdom. Our God knows the problems we face. The burdens we carry. He understands that we are easily discouraged when difficulties pile up and the road ahead seems littered with impossibilities.

And so, He goes on to further open the conversation:

> Call to Me, and I will answer you, and show you great and mighty things, which you do not know (Jeremiah 33:3).

Quite an offer! Especially when we consider the Hebrew root of the word translated as "mighty." It means inaccessible or beyond human understanding.

I don't know about you, but every day I have a long list of problems and challenges where the answers seem inaccessible. I want to decide what's best for all concerned but often I have to admit I'm stumped.

Then God opens the conversation of prayer by promising that if I take time alone with Him, He will give me insight and discernment, plus a strategy and courage way beyond anything I could think up myself. St. Patrick said, "Belong to God and become a wonder to yourself." It happens. I discover answers in prayer that astound me and I exclaim, "I could never have thought that up myself!"

Remembering those times makes God's invitation to conversation a very welcome one as I prepare for prayer. When I'm under a pile of problems, His encouraging conversation starter, "Call on Me, I'll show you things you'd never conceive of by yourself," creates an urgent desire to pray.

Another way God opens the conversation of prayer on days when we are loaded down with problems are His words from Psalm 46:10, "Be still, and know that I am God." "Be still" means more than silence. The words can also mean, "Let up, leave off, let go." In other words, "Let go of your tight grip. I am your God. I will help you." Irresistibly we want to talk to Him in response to His gracious offer.

Sometimes we feel reluctant to pray because of some failures in our lives. When we need God the most, we resist the conversation of prayer because we feel unworthy. At times like that the Lord's invitation is articulated in verses of great assurance of grace. Take Isaiah 43:25 for example:

> I, even I, am He who blots out your transgressions for My own sake; and I will not remember your sins.

We know what that Old Testament promise cost God in the death of His Son. It is through Christ, the Mediator, that we are called to prayer. And we respond with the awesome realization that we are loved and already forgiven.

The message of Christ is filled with invitations to prayer. He comes to us and says,

> Behold, I stand at the door and knock. If anyone hears My voice and opens the door, I will come in to him and dine with him, and he with Me (Revelation 3:20).

What an impelling call to prayer! And what a vivid description of the personal exchange prayer is meant to be.

All Christ needs is access, and He will come in to make our conversation possible as the eternal Mediator. He calls it "dining" with us, and we with Him. In biblical parlance the common evening meal suggests intimate and joyous fellowship. This is what He envisions prayer to be: an intimate communication in which He is completely open with us and we can be our authentic selves with Him. A free and natural exchange can take place. Nothing is so healing and empowering as the quiet, uninterrupted communication with God through His Son and inspired by His Spirit.

Years ago, I discovered a transforming truth about prayer. Up to that time I thought of prayer only as a means of receiving guidance and power to work *for* God. Then I came across a statement by

Thomas Chalmers, a great Scots preacher of a previous generation. During a prolonged illness, he discovered this truth: "Prayer does not enable us to do a greater work for God. Prayer *is* a greater work for God."

Prayer is the greatest work we can do for God because when we pray we receive His most wondrous gift: communion with Him. Mother Teresa of Calcutta put it clearly, "Prayer enlarges the heart until it is capable of containing God's gift of Himself."

How Shall We Respond?

And how shall we respond to this gracious invitation? What is our answer as our part of preparation for a conversation with God? It is simply to tell Him how much we need Him and want to be with Him.

Again the Scriptures help us. They free us to express our longing to be alone with God and how thankful we are that He has initiated the conversation. So often I feel like the psalmist:

> As the deer pants for the water brooks, so pants my soul for You, O God. My soul thirsts for God, for the living God (Psalm 42:1-2).

A dominant desire like that not only pleases God but dilates our total consciousness to an attentive conversation with Him. He gives His best to those who want Him most.

> Fear not, for I am with you; be not dismayed, for I am your God. I will strengthen you, yes, I will help you, I will uphold you with My righteous right hand (Isaiah 41:10).

Sometimes my response to God's invitation for a conversation of prayer is to rally every part of my being to wide-awake alertness to the privilege. All of Psalm 103 helps me do that, especially the first five verses:

> Bless the LORD, O my soul; and all that is within me, bless His holy name! Bless the LORD, O my soul, and forget not all His

benefits; who forgives all your iniquities, who heals all your diseases, who redeems your life from destruction, who crowns you with lovingkindness and tender mercies, who satisfies your mouth with good things, so that your youth is renewed like the eagle's.

That wake-up call to my whole self—mind, soul, and body—prepares me to put into my own words my personal response to God and to His outstretched heart. It goes something like this, "Father, I am stunned and amazed again and again by Your initiative love in calling me into a conversation of prayer. I'm so thankful. You knew how much I needed to break the silence barrier; You understand my hurts and hopes; You are sensitive to the fact that I need You more than my next breath. I accept with awe and wonder Your offer to talk with me and allow me to open my heart to You. I have no righteousness of my own to deserve this privilege, but accept it only in the righteousness You purchased for me through Jesus Christ, Your Son, and my Lord. With Him to guide me, and Your Spirit within to inspire me, I will listen to You with rapt attention and respond with all my mind, heart, and will. I love You, Father."

All of this is prelude to the subsequent steps of a conversation with God. The Scriptures I have suggested for this initial step of preparation are only a few of the hundreds in the Bible. Over the years, I have tried to memorize many of them. They help me claim God's invitations to prayer. Most of all, they remind me that prayer always starts at His instigation.

A
Conversation
of Love

We wait, quietly basking in the sheer wonder of being called into a conversation of prayer with God. Then He speaks and calls us on to the next phase of prayer. His words echo down the centuries and reverberate in our souls.

> Let not the wise man glory in his wisdom, let not the mighty man glory in his might, nor let the rich man glory in his riches; but let him who glories glory in this, that he understands and knows Me, that I am the LORD, exercising lovingkindness, judgment, and righteousness in the earth. For in these I delight (Jeremiah 9:23-24).

The supreme glory of our life is to understand and know God! The more we know God, the more we praise Him; and the more we praise Him, the more we know Him.

Praise should be distinguished from thanksgiving.

When we give thanks, we glorify God for what He has done; when we praise Him, we glorify Him for what He is in Himself.

Praise concentrates on God for Himself rather than His gifts and provisions. And according to His own desires expressed so clearly, He longs for us to glory in the fact that we understand and know Him. The depth of our praise measures the quality of our relationship with Him.

The psalmist expressed genuine praise when he said,

> I will praise you, O LORD, with my whole heart; I will tell of Your marvelous works. I will be glad and rejoice in You; I will sing praises to Your name (Psalm 9:1-2).

In Psalm 63:3-4 the same authentic praise is expressed:

> Because Your lovingkindness is better than life, my lips shall praise You. Thus I will bless You while I live.

In both of these verses, the psalmist is riveted on God.

True Praise Is Difficult

For many people, profound and prolonged praise is very difficult. They don't know God all that well personally. So they quickly move through praise and on to telling God of their needs. Unselfish praise, self-forgetting glorification of God for His majesty and grace, comes harder.

There's also a deeper reason: Praise is the antidote for pride. And pride does not give up its grip easily. When we praise God, we admit He is Lord of all. Years ago, as a student, I memorized some lines that make my mind and heart soar in praise: "God is a Spirit, infinite, eternal and unchangeable; in His being are wisdom, power, holiness, and truth." Now, I add grace. Or take what God Himself said in His call to praise from Jeremiah, "But let him glory in this, that he understands and knows Me" and pay attention to what He wants us to know— "that I am the Lord, exercising lovingkindness, judgement, and righteousness in the earth." Our God delights in those who know these attributes of His nature.

God desires an intimate, personal relationship with us. Praise surges from our hearts for what He is to us in that relationship, quite apart from what He provides for us.

We can understand that on a human level of relationship. Being loved only because of what we do for people wears thin. "Who loves and praises me for what I am?" we ask.

Praise for the Triune God

Praising God for who He is leads us to adoration for the magnificent ways He has of being God—as Father, Son, and Holy Spirit. This is a mystery, yes, but don't forget that the word mystery in Greek, *mysterion,* is not something enigmatic, inexplicable, inscrutable, or beyond explanation. Rather, it is that which can be known only by divine revelation. We think of a mystery as knowledge withheld; when it comes to the Trinity, it is truth revealed. And God has chosen it to reveal His wondrous nature so we can love and praise Him.

We can understand and know God only as He chooses to reveal His attributes of lovingkindness, justice, and righteousness. All three persons or subsistencies of God have acted in perfect harmony and oneness in Creation, the Incarnation, the Atonement of the Cross, the Resurrection, and the birth of a new creation of humankind at Pentecost. We know who God is by His self-disclosure in history.

We were created for praise. When what was meant to be our instinctive natural adoration was debilitated at the core of our nature by sin, the Father sent Christ to redeem us so that we would be able to "understand and know" Him. Unfettered praise leaps with joy in us when we accept the staggering truth:

> And the Word became flesh and dwelt among us, and we beheld His glory, the glory of the only begotten of the Father, full of grace and truth...And of His fullness we have all received, and grace for grace (John 1:14,16).

In Christ's life, message, death, and resurrection, we behold the revelation of God's lovingkindness, judgment, and righteousness dramatized and displayed before our eyes.

"I am the way, the truth, and the life. No one comes to the Father except through Me," He boldly claimed. "He who has seen Me has seen the Father" (John 14:6,9).

Then stand at the foot of the cross and your praise will surge. Through Christ's death, God was both the *just* and the *justifier* (Romans 3:26). And who can contain his praise at the empty tomb or when the risen Christ tells us, "Because I live you shall live also"? Surely that's enough to keep us praising through eternity.

But that's not all. The risen Christ is also the baptizer with the Holy Spirit. What would we do without the daily infilling of the Holy Spirit who guides, enables, and empowers? He inspires our growth in Christlikeness through His fruit, equips us for ministry with His gifts, and enables supernatural living through His power. But the Holy Spirit does not draw attention to Himself: His ministry is to help us glorify the risen Christ.

We learn how to praise from the way the Father loves and honors His Son, the way the Son glorifies the Father, and the way the Holy Spirit exalts the Son in our lives. It's a glory circle of love. So we join the apostle Paul in bursting into adoration for "The grace of the Lord Jesus Christ, and the love of God, and the communion of the Holy Spirit" (2 Corinthians 13:14).

The Secret of Praise

When you or I are called into prayer, the living Christ, through the power of the Spirit, enables our praise to the Father. We do not produce praise on our own, alone; Christ motivates it and the Spirit manifests it in our hearts.

It is so crucial to appreciate this dynamic of true worship as we move on from preparation to actually praising God. We must overcome the duality of our thinking. Customarily, we think of God "up there" or "out there somewhere." We think of praise as something we do from a distance with our own strength. But our moods vacillate; our attitudes fluctuate. We don't always "feel" like praising God.

This is why we need the Mediator, Christ our Lord, to reaffirm our relationship with the Father. "To Him [the Father] be glory in the church *by* Christ Jesus throughout all ages" (Ephesians 3:21). He is the rallier—the cheerleader, if you please, of praise.

So true praise is done *through* us not just *by* us. What is our part? To yield! We were fashioned, redeemed, and recreated to be channels of praise. When our conversation of prayer moves into praise, at that moment we can be led in our adoration of the Father *for who He is*, by the Spirit of Christ. And His call to worship is:

> The hour is coming, and now is, when the true worshippers will worship the Father in spirit and truth; for the Father is seeking such to worship Him. God is Spirit, and those who worship Him must worship in spirit and truth (John 4:23-24).

Our spirit is the highest part of our nature. True worship happens when our spirit is yielded and is ushered by Christ into friendship and intimacy with the Father. The immortal and invisible dimension of our being is brought into the presence of the immortal and invisible God.

Ask for the Power to Praise

I've found it essential to ask for the power to praise: "Holy Father, I want to glory only in understanding and knowing You. I surrender my mind, emotions, will, and body for Your Son and the Holy Spirit to usher me into Your glory circle so that I will be included in the loop of love You share. I want to glorify You with my praise!"

That prayer may sound presumptuous. Not at all! It is simply claiming what Christ prayed on the night before He was crucified. His petition of the Father puts into perspective the purpose of His incarnation and His continuing ministry. I listen in on His prayer with awe; it gives me holy audacity to praise.

> I do not pray for these alone [the disciples], but also for those who will believe in Me through their word [you and me]; that

they may be one, as You, Father, are in Me, and I in You.... that they may be one just as We are one: I in them, and You in Me; that they may be made perfect in one, and that the world may know that You have sent Me, and have loved them as You have loved Me. Father, I desire that they also whom You gave Me may be with Me where I am, that they may behold My glory which You have given Me; for You loved Me before the foundation of the world. O righteous Father! The world has not known You, but I have known You; and these have known that You sent Me. And I have declared to them Your name and will declare it [through history, but now to you and me!], that the love with which You loved Me may be in them, and I in them (John 17:20-26).

As I have stated in my books through the years, Christ is the heart of God. Through the Spirit He brings our hearts into union with the heart of God. It's in that union that we offer our praise. Thinking magnificently of God unleashes our praise. So, don't hurry through praise. All the other steps of our conversation with God in prayer depend on the fellowship with God it produces.

How to Start Praising

Now, yielded as a channel of praise, begin by telling God how much you love Him. Say it now as you read this: "I love you, Lord, and I want to tell You why. I love You for who You are." Imagine the delight of the Father as you share the joy of what He has meant to you! He knows us and wants us to know Him.

I will never forget a conversation with one of my sons. He had asked me to set aside a time when we could talk. When we sat down, I was fearful that there was some great problem or some misunderstanding between us that needed to be straightened out. To my great delight he said, "Dad, there's so much I never told you about what you mean to me. Not what you've done for me, but who you are. I just want you to sit quietly without getting embarrassed or interrupting while I tell you why I love you."

In spite of all my perceived inadequacies as a parent and a person, I was thrilled to sense that he knew me and had observed some of the result of the Potter with the human clay of my life. And he also knows the work still to be done on the Potter's wheel.

A similar delight was given me when, as part of my church's twentieth anniversary celebration of my ministry with them, my three children wrote a "Dear Dad" letter and had it printed in the church newspaper without my knowledge. I sobbed with pure joy as I read this letter of love. But again, the thing that moved me so deeply was that they understood and knew the passion, vision, and verve of my life. They, more than anyone (except my late wife, Mary Jane), knew my weaknesses, but they also knew something else—the longing of my heart to live for God with gusto and joy.

These "how much more" illustrations only touch the fringe of what our praise means to God. He has no imperfections for us to overlook while giving affirmation, so how much more is God pleased when we reveal in our praise that we understand and know Him, and glory in that alone!

Use of Scripture in Praise

The Scriptures are invaluable in finding words to express our praise. And on this side of Calvary and Pentecost, we pray them to God with even greater depth of praise.

My beloved professor, James Stewart, taught me how to use the psalms as the same praise guide used by Jesus. He said, "All the way through the Book of Psalms, even in its most sorrow-ladened passages, you feel that you are walking on a smoldering volcano of praise, liable to burst out at any moment into a great flame of praise to God. And as the book draws to a close, the flame leaps clear from the smoke; here you have praise, and nothing but praise."

The psalmist gives us our motto for praise:

> Praise the LORD! Praise the LORD, O my soul! While I live I will praise the LORD; I will sing praises to my God while I have my being (Psalm 146:1).

Memorize that. Pray it every day as part of your praise. The psalmist wanted to praise the Lord as long as he was alive. A great commitment for us, too. Especially when we realize that in heaven the angels, the company of heaven, and all our departed loved ones who began their eternal life here through faith in Christ, are involved in continual praise. We'll find it rather uncomfortable if we don't learn to praise during this earthly phase of our eternal life. What's more, when we praise we have a foretaste of true joy, the ecstasy of heaven.

John Donne saw praising God now as training for praising Him in heaven:

> Since I am coming to that holy room
> Where, with a quire of saints forevermore,
> I shall be made Thy music; as I come
> I tune the instrument at the door,
> And what I must do then, think here before.

The psalms I find most stimulating to my own personal prayers are those in which the psalmist uses the first-person singular in giving praise to God. I like to use them as a responsive reading in which I reword the verse or passage as my own personal expression.

Take for example Psalm 108:1. It's an especially good response to the call to praise that God gave us in Jeremiah 9:24: "But let him who glories, glory in this...that I am the LORD."

Verse of praise:
O God, my heart is steadfast; I will sing and give praise, even with my glory (Psalm 108:1).

Response:
O God, that's how I feel. My heart is firm in praise of You. I will not squander my ability to glorify on anything or anyone else. I praise You, Lord, all You are.

Singing our praises is liberating. Follow the admonition, "Praise the LORD! Sing to the LORD a new song" (Psalm 149:1). New songs come from fresh discoveries of the greatness of God. Sing out your own lines that express your new insights of His majesty. Don't worry about the rhythm or the music—and if you're like me, don't be concerned about the pitch. Sometimes it's good to just sing, "I praise You, Lord; I love You, Lord; I glorify You, Lord; I worship You, Lord!" And then just sing on about the nature of God, His attributes, your new discoveries of His grace.

The great praise hymns also give us words to sing our praises. And a contemporary praise song I often use in personal prayer goes,

> I love You, Lord, and I lift my voice,
> To worship You, O my soul, rejoice!
> Take joy, my King, in what You hear;
> May it be a sweet, sweet sound in Your ear.*

Many times, even the Scripture's praise and my own said or sung words seem inadequate to express all the praise I feel. I'm thankful that the Holy Spirit who knows my heart can maximize my fumbling words and wing them to the heart of God. The Spirit reveals more of the mystery and wonder of God and helps me praise Him with even greater exaltation.

Paul experienced this gift of praise from the Holy Spirit. He shared his discovery with the Corinthians by quoting Isaiah 64:4 and 65:17, and then he explained what these verses mean for the praising Christian.

> "Eye has not seen, nor ear heard, nor have entered into the heart of man the things which God has prepared for those who love Him." But God has revealed them through His Spirit. For the Spirit searches all things, yes, even the deep things of God. For what man knows the things of a man which is in him? Even so no one knows the things of God except the Spirit of God. Now we have received, not the spirit of the world, but the Spirit who is from God, that we might know the things that have been freely given to us by God (1 Corinthians 2:9-12).

---

* Laurie Klein, "I Love You, Lord" (House of Mercy, Maranatha Music, 1980).

Claiming this ministry of the Spirit, I have felt deeper stirrings of praise than my own words can express. I feel the Spirit praising through me. Sometimes when I am quiet afterward, I am given deeper insight into the mystery of God's wondrous nature and His plans for me. The result is an indescribable joy in God Himself that changes me.

Praise Changes Us

The old saying, "Prayer changes things," is only half true. What it also changes is our attitudes as we relinquish our worries and anxieties to the Lord. Often, then, when we leave the results to Him, He intervenes and does what we could not do. Also, prayer changes our perception of what is possible and recruits us to be part of the solution, not part of the problem.

And it's during the step of praise in our prayers that we experience relinquishment. You cannot really praise the Lord of all and keep control of all at the same time. With praise in times of difficulty, dark moods are lifted; our troubled spirits are transformed; and our unwilling hearts are made receptive. Plus I find that bright times of success and smooth sailing are elevated with praise into joy. But whatever the circumstances of life, praise brings us to the heart of God.

I've experienced that repeatedly. When I'm busy or loaded down with concerns, my temptation is to rush past praise and get to telling the Lord what I think He ought to do. It doesn't work. When I take time to magnify the Lord—that is, expand my understanding and knowledge of the Lord, for who could expand the majesty of God—I am much more ready to receive His wisdom and power when He moves the conversation of prayer on to specifics.

The ancient English word for worship, "weorthscipe," or worthy-shape, meant to establish the worth, the wonder, and glory of God in our minds and hearts. Praise is a vital opening phase of prayer. Without it, prayer is talking circles around the perpendicular pronoun: "I"; with it, we do what God has asked—that we glory in Him.

4

The Conversation Deepens

Our praise subsides into quiet adoration.

Then silence.

We have beheld the glory and holiness of God. The heights of our adoration have made us aware of the depths of our need. Our mistakes, failures, and sins now make us feel uncomfortable in His presence. The more we sense His love, the more we feel distressed by the repetitive patterns of our lives that stand in the way of being faithful and obedient to Him first in our lives.

Now God breaks the silence and leads us on to the next step of conversation with Him. Listen:

> If My people who are called by My name will humble themselves, and pray and seek My face, and turn from their wicked ways, then I will hear from heaven, and will forgive their sin and heal their land (2 Chronicles 7:14).

With the words of this ancient promise first made to Solomon at the time of the dedication of the temple, the Lord calls us to confession, the third phase of prayer. Here again He leads the conversation. We sense that He intends to go deeper in our confession than we have ever experienced.

We tend to think of confession as our act of setting things right with God by telling Him the things we think are our sins. We've missed the real meaning of confession. In Hebrew, *confession* means to "show, point out, or acknowledge." And that's God's prerogative. In Greek, the word is *homologeo*, "To say after."

Authentic confession is to allow the Lord to press to the deepest levels of our lives and point out what He wants us to confess. So often we tell Him about our surface failures. He digs deeper into the motives and habits of our hearts.

That's why the Lord has called us to humble ourselves and confess our wicked ways. We can appreciate the need to humble ourselves and seek His face, His presence, but the words *wicked ways* sound very severe to our contemporary ears. The word *wicked* means habitual, repetitive sin. Sin is missing the mark; for us, the bull's-eye is profound fellowship with God. And sin is not merely the little peccadillos with which we complicate our lives. God is most concerned about what is in our deeper hearts that separates us from Him.

It is an awesome, disturbing experience to ask God to show us our real selves. Confession is to say, "Lord, show me anything You see that is consistently blocking my relationship with You." The heart of the issue is *our hearts*. And God knows what's really going on in our hearts. "Would not God search this out? For He knows the secrets of the heart" (Psalm 44:21).

Idols of the Heart

He also knows the idols of our hearts. He knows that these idols are what cause our persistent spiritual problems. This is the particular proclivity of religious people who repeat surface prayers of confession, but do not experience forgiveness and liberation. People like you and me.

Down through the ages, God's people have perpetuated the division between what they pray and what's in their hearts. To twist a phrase: There's many a slip 'twixt the *heart* and the lip! And God says,

These people draw near with their mouths, and honor Me with their lips, but have removed their hearts far from Me (Isaiah 29:13).

That gives us pause in our conversation with God. It is both alarming and reassuring to realize that He knows all about what's in our hearts anyway. And we suspect the true peace we long for will come only if we say after Him what He wants us to confess. We are given the courage to say,

Search all my sense, and know my heart
Who only can make known
And let the deep, the hidden part
To me be fully shown.

God's response to that prayer may be more than we bargained for. When the Israelites went into exile in Babylon, the prophet Ezekiel was sent to tell the people to repent and turn away from embracing the foreign idols of their captors. Even the leaders of God's chosen people were participating in idolatry and apostasy. He also speaks to us the words He gave Ezekiel to say to the elders of Israel:

Everyone...who sets up his idols in his heart, and puts before him what causes him to stumble into iniquity...I the Lord will answer him who comes, according to the multitude of his idols, that I may seize...their heart, because they are estranged from Me by their idols (Ezekiel 14:4-5).

The abbreviated text makes this a direct challenge for us. We know the problem Israel had worshiping idols, but I feel led to keep sight of the important implication of God's words for the idols that have captured our own hearts today. Loyalty to them causes our repetitive sins of commission and omission that we repeatedly confess but continue to do. *We don't have to spend our lives in bondage to repetitive patterns.*

God, the Iconoclast

Our God is an eternal iconoclast. He persistently exposes the false idols, distorted beliefs, and confused loyalties to religious institutions that vie for first place in our hearts. He will not allow us to gloss over any of His commandments, especially the first two. As the Divine Iconoclast, God abhors syncretism, the worship of more than one god. Israel dabbled in the worship of Baal and gave allegiance to foreign gods of other nations. They wanted Yahweh *plus* other gods. Such idolatry is still around.

God created us for Himself and will not accept second place to other gods or the graven images we make for them. Especially when the sanctuary for the worship of these idols is in what we think is the privacy of our own hearts.

What are these idols? When we allow God to lead our confession, He gets down to business.

The Idol of Pride

The idol of pride looms above all the other idols of our hearts. It demands the false worship of what earlier we called the perpendicular pronoun. Pride is bordering life on the north, south, east, and west with our control, our plans, our desires, our will! It is the original sin—wanting to be our own gods and run our own lives. Oh, to be sure, we syncretize the worship of self with the worship of God. And that's what causes disturbance in our hearts. We become a walking civil war.

C.S. Lewis wrote about the dictatorship of pride. It wants to win the civil war, with our egos on the throne of our hearts. Pride is a discontented general of the rebel troops of our desires and ambitions. This idol is basically selfish: It wants all the credit. Mark Twain was partially right: "Temper is what gets you into trouble; pride is what keeps you there." I would say that pride infects our temper, and keeps us in constant battles for our rights and our demand to be recognized.

The infection of pride is insidious. It grows in us and constantly expands. Alexander Solzhenitsyn vividly observed this. "Pride," he wrote, "grows in the human heart like lard on a pig"!

Here's a good example. There was a frog who envied the ability of geese to fly. One day he convinced two geese to put a strong stick between their beaks. He told them that they could fly in close formation with the stick firmly between them. Then, with his mouth, he firmly grabbed the stick and the geese took off.

The frog was flying! The first to defy the law of gravity. However, when the geese flew over a village, the people looked up in amazement. "What a clever frog!" they exclaimed. "We've never seen a frog fly before. Whoever devised such an ingenious way for a frog to fly?"

The frog could not resist the impulse of pride. He opened his mouth and said, "I did!...Ahhhhhhhh!" Opening his mouth to claim the applause, he let go of his clenched-mouth grip on the stick. Pride went before his fall.

When the actress Sarah Bernhardt performed in Paris, everything was organized around her. After the audiences had jammed the theater and sat waiting for her performance, the stage manager would go to her dressing room and say with oily solicitousness, "Madam, it will be eight o'clock whenever it suits you."

Wouldn't it be great to have life organized around our whims? We try—in subtle and sometimes very imperious ways. We'd like to be the author, director, scene designer, and star performer in the drama of our lives. If we could only get all the people in our lives to play the bit parts and have God in the audience, not as the producer and director.

We think the opposite of pride is humility. And yet how quickly we become proud of being humble. Pride is a poison that pervades our being. It requires a daily antidote. The purging of the antidote is radical. It begins its work when we confess to God that pride is an idol in our hearts. Then comes the surrender of our lives. But finally only Christ can break the power-bind of pride. It's a miracle of His grace. Pride is really trying to fill our emptiness with self-love. When we experience His unqualified love from the cross and the cleansing power of His blood purges us, only then can we let Him throw down and crush the idol of pride.

Allow the Holy Spirit to show you the ways the idol of pride is erected repeatedly in your own heart. Remember, confession is to say after Him what He reveals we need to admit before God. A.W. Tozer used to say, "Nothing will or can restore order until our hearts make one decision: God shall be exalted above all else."

The Idol of Perfectionism

Very close to the idol of pride in our hearts stands the idol of perfectionism. Really, it's another form of pride. Perfectionism is the self-effort to be worthy of God's election, call, and affirmation. Augustine said, "This is the perfection of a man, to find out his imperfections." I agree. It is the finding out of our own imperfections that leads us to confession. But so often it doesn't: We simply try harder to be adequate, good on our own strength. C.H. Spurgeon put it bluntly, "He who boasts of being perfect is perfect in folly. I never saw a perfect man!"

We think of a perfectionist as a person who always has to have everything according to his or her design, one who fastidiously strives to never make a mistake.

The idol of perfectionism is actually much more demanding than that. It's really the problem of self-atonement. Pride may cause self-aggrandizement; perfectionism causes self-justification. Perfectionism sneaks around Golgotha. Something must be added to the substitutionary sacrifice of the cross! It's very difficult for us to imagine that we don't have to do or be something more in order to be accepted by God. Spiritual perfectionism is uneasy with justification by faith alone and life lived totally dependent on grace.

Perfectionism grows its own kind of legalism. Rules and dicta, regulations and requirements are its security. "Do this and you will be loved," is its motto. It results in uncreative guilt and, equally serious, it produces a judgmental attitude and criticism of others. No one can please us because we are not pleased with ourselves. And that inner displeasure is caused by the panic of not measuring up to our own demanding standards.

Now you may not think of yourself as a perfectionist in the traditional sense. But do you ever entertain the notion that God will love you more if you are good in every way? Or the flip side of that: Do you ever feel He can't love you because of something you've done?

When the Lord takes over and guides our confession, He exposes this idol of perfectionism and explores all of its causes. He reminds us that we are already loved, forgiven, and accepted through the cross. Nothing needs to be added. He shows us that the problem of our perfectionism is that our standards are too low, not too high. He calls us to be perfect on a higher level. "You shall be perfect," says Christ, "just as your Father in heaven is perfect" (Matthew 5:48). Here the word *perfect* means "fully mature," to achieve the purpose or goal of our lives. This verse completes the section of the Sermon on the Mount in which Jesus called us to serve others, love, and forgive. Christ Himself is our example of perfection. The life He lived as Jesus of Nazareth is the life He now seeks to enable in us through the indwelling power of the Holy Spirit. We can't do it alone. Maturity is a miracle.

Our willingness to be led in confession brings us to the need to admit our self-generated perfectionism that is based on only our limited idea of what is possible. And from that deeper confession comes release from the bonds of the sins of self-condemnation, restless dissatisfaction with ourselves and others, and our negative attitudes about life.

God wants to heal our obsession with shame. It is ingrained in our nature by parents and culture. Shame has been used as a whip to lash us into obedience. The "Shame on you!" from others becomes, "Shame on me!" And then Christ intervenes, "I took all the shame on Calvary! Now you can be motivated by My once-and-for-all, never-needs-to-be-repeated atonement. My love is your motivation, and when you fail—forgiveness is given even before you ask."

Again, we are ready for confession of what our perfectionism and resultant shame have done to us, and by us to others, to rob us of freedom, joy, and the power to love ourselves and others in a healthy and creative way.

The Idol of Piety

The idol of piety holds hands with the idol of perfectionism. Sometimes it hides behind perfectionism. The classical definition of *piety* is "devotion to religion." In some periods of history it had a positive meaning, describing a person who is wholeheartedly devoted to God. Most often in our day, however, piety is devotion to *human* standards of theological orthodoxy or religious practices that become diminutive gods in our hearts. This kind of piety leads to superiority and exclusiveness. We think of ourselves as among the chosen few—usually a very few.

The idol of piety can be a demanding false god in denominationalism that thinks "our way is the only right way"; in orthodox fundamentalism that finds its security in a set of beliefs, rather than in Christ; in the charismatic who becomes rigid about speaking in tongues as the only evidence that a person has been baptized by the Holy Spirit; or in the social activist who judges other people's servanthood.

A student asked Karl Barth, "In what religions has God revealed Himself?" Barth replied incisively, "God has not revealed Himself in any religion, not even Christianity. He has only revealed Himself in Christ, the Mediator."

That statement requires some reflection. When the forms and structures and traditions become more important than Christ, then whatever brand of Christianity we espouse becomes an idol. Christ is the Mediator, *not* the religious customs men and women have built up through the years.

And yet, we find so much false security in our theology, our kind of church, our jargon. Group pressure to conform also becomes very important to us. People withhold acceptance until we sing their song to their tune. And we catch ourselves doing the same thing.

What causes it? Well, all of us are really very insecure. We gravitate to the secondary security of our religions and to those of like-mind to overcome our loneliness. That becomes an idol in our hearts when it is substituted for the security only God Himself can give us in His Son and in His Spirit.

I need to rediscover this true security often. I pastored a church that drew people from many different backgrounds, and my media ministry reached people from across a broad spectrum of religious beliefs, including secular humanism. People wanted to categorize me in some camp. Or they wanted to straighten out my theology until it was acceptable to their persuasion. Now, as then, I must daily reaffirm my security in Christ alone. But also, I must check myself to be sure I'm not rigidly pious about religion. I want all that God offers, all that the Scriptures promise, all of the power available in Christ and through the Holy Spirit. Often I have to confess the bogus security I think is in my own position, or in being accepted by someone else.

What about you? Does your devotion to religion, a denomination, some particular theological camp, or antique traditions ever become inordinately important? When they do, the Lord leads us to confession of our misplaced loyalty.

The Idol of the Past

The idol of the past demands constant oblations of misplaced worship. We dote on what we've accomplished. Our education, positions, titles, and achievements are arranged carefully before this idol in our hearts. We become obsessed with yesterday. It is rooted in fear of the future and the mistaken belief that what lies ahead will never equal what we knew in the past.

One of the most debilitating anchors in the mud is our cherished memories of our previous experiences of God. Does that surprise you? What I mean is, our experience of God in the present and in the future is more important than idolizing our experiences of Him in the past. Of course, we'll never forget the day we became Christians, or when we experienced a special empowering for some great challenge or opportunity. I'm not talking about *forgetting* evidences of the Lord's grace in the past; I am talking about focusing our thinking into a vibrant expectation of what God will do, reveal, and enable in the present and the future!

And here's a question that gives me pause: Am I more excited about my own plans and projects for the future than I am about the fresh experiences of God that tomorrow holds? How would you answer? Careful how you answer. Which do you think about most when you contemplate the future? Is God merely an addendum to what you already have planned?

God says, "Behold, I will do a new thing" (Isaiah 43:19). And we respond, "Lord, forgive me when I idolize the past. I confess my lack of expectancy for fresh experiences of You: Your power, truth, and interventions. I pull my anchor out of the mud and lift my sails to be filled with the wind of your Spirit."

Idols of People and Popularity

The idols of people and popularity are Siamese twins. They are attached and seem inseparable.

People are important to us. Sometimes they become more important to us than God. Or at least that's the way we act at times. Often, the potential loss of loved ones or friends brings more than healthy grief; it throws us into panic. We can't bear the thought of life without them.

Jack Paar, a famous television personality and the original host of the *Tonight Show*, really admired Fred Allen. One day he said, "Fred, you are my god!" Quicker than a wink, Allen shot back, "There are five thousand churches in New York, and you have to be an atheist!"

Allen was right. No one can take the place of God in our lives.

He wants to set us free from our desperate need for people so that we can truly love and serve them.

On a daily basis we realize how much we need the approval of people. Rejection of any kind throws us into a tailspin. We harbor the bitter memories of slights and oversights, harsh or cutting criticism.

And we all long to be popular. Dwight Eisenhower once said, "Popularity is like sweet perfume. It's fine if you don't swallow it." But some of us not only swallow it, we become addicted to it. The danger lies in how we are tempted to compromise to keep a steady flow of it.

The Lord never promised that we would always win popularity contests or be "number one." What He did promise was to give us the power to love others profoundly and speak the truth with love.

The issue for our prayers of confession is to honestly ask the Lord to show us when we have needed people so much that they have competed for first place in our hearts. If we are open, He will reveal to us when we have compromised our faith for popularity.

Also, because He loves us so much, our Lord gently touches the festering boils of our hurts and painful memories. If we ask Him, He will lance them and draw out the ache with the poultice of His grace.

The Idol of Possessions

Defenses go up whenever the Lord asks us about the idol of our possessions. The American culture has put such an emphasis on things! The entire science of marketing and advertising has been developed to discover what will appeal to the emptiness in our hearts. The world says acquiring things and accumulating money can fulfill our purpose in living.

Have you seen the bumper stickers and T-shirts that proclaim, "Whoever dies with the most toys—wins!"

This is the idol of money and what it can buy; the things we have acquired with it, and what they come to mean to us; the worry we have over earning enough of it to make ends meet or keeping a little of what we have. Money and our possessions become an idol when we lose the conviction or forget that everything we have and all that we are belongs to the Lord.

The only way to break the mammon membrane around our souls is to praise God daily for appointing us as stewards over what He has enabled us to acquire. He is also Lord of our expenditures.

The biblical mandate is tithing. The first tenth of what we earn is not ours. It is to be used for the Lord's work in the world through the church and parachurch ministries for evangelism, missions, and care for the poor and hungry. Tithers budget their expenditures from nine-tenths of their income. The tithe comes off the top, not after we have taken care of everything else.

A man wrote to me, "Every time I start to tithe, some big financial crisis occurs—the car needs a couple of hundred dollars' worth of work, or someone breaks something of mine and it needs to be replaced, and tithing goes out the window. God doesn't seem to send me the money for either, and I feel like a stepchild when I try to be obedient. What's wrong?"

The man is facing that hard choice to "Tithe off the top" and not even think of that ten percent as expendable income. If he thinks he can draw on his tithing account for personal expenses, he's not yet begun to tithe. In a sense, he is embezzling from God! When he stuck to his decision, God did help him budget the other nine-tenths and is surprising him with extra, unanticipated money.

One of the most courageous things we can do in our daily conversations alone with God is to ask Him to take our spiritual pulse to see if worry over money and our possessions is causing an acceleration of our pulse beat. If it is, He will show us the deeper cause and also guide us to solutions we could not have dreamed up ourselves. The idol of possessions causes anxiety. Confessing that to Him brings forgiveness and the power for us to live as His stewards of all that is really His and what He has entrusted to us to use as long as we give Him the glory.

The Idol of Presumption

One last idol in our hearts is now confronted by our Lord. It is the idol of presumption. This idol permits all the things we do and say which we know will break the heart of God, but which we go ahead and do anyway. We do and say these things presuming on His loving kindness and forgiveness. In Hebrew, the word *presumption* means an arrogant denial of the laws of God. In Greek, it means "daring" with a negative connotation, used in conjunction with "self-willed."

In this category of sin the Lord leads us to confess all the sins of commission and omission we do, knowing all the time they are wrong. These are trespasses, *paraptoma* in Greek, a false step, a blunder, a falling away or aside, a deviation from righteousness and truth. We fall away from God's best for us when we hurt others, commit character assassination with gossip, say less or more than the truth in any relationship, express envy or jealousy, express uncontrolled anger, neglect the physical needs of the poor and hungry, or abuse our own or another person's sexuality in thought or action. This list goes on and on. In short, presumptuous sins are those we do willfully, while falsely thinking it doesn't really matter.

In this confession portion of our conversation with God, we discover He knows all about us, and what we have done and said *does* matter. He brings these things to light so we can confess them. The sure sign that we have grappled with the idol of presumption and have received forgiveness comes when we can pray with the psalmist with deep resolve, "Keep back your servant also from presumptuous sins; let them not have dominion over me" (Psalm 19:13).

Assurance of Pardon

God has led us through traumatic confrontations with the idols of our hearts to expose the deeper causes of the sins He has guided us to confess. Now the Mediator, Christ the Lord, assures us of the pardon we urgently need. It is the pardon for which He gave His life with inexpressible suffering to reconcile us to the Father. With authority and power He says, "Your sins are forgiven!"

And in response we claim the wondrous gift, saying Paul's words in Colossians 2:13b-14 in the most personal way,

> Christ has made me alive together with Him, having forgiven me all trespasses, having wiped out the handwriting of requirements that was against me....And He has taken it out of the way, having nailed it to the cross.

In Greek cities like Colosse, when a person committed an offense or owed a great debt, the charges were written out and posted in the city square for all to see. The parchment was made of vellum, which the ink did not penetrate. When the offense was exonerated or the debt paid, the charges were wiped away. Another way of declaring that the offender was free was to drive a nail through the charge list.

Both have been done for us. The slate is wiped clean. The charge list of our trespasses has been nailed to the cross of Calvary, our lasting assurance of pardon.

What can we say? William Cowper gave us lines to match our new resolve:

> The dearest idol I have known
> Whatever that idol be
> Help me to tear it from Thy throne
> And worship only Thee.

5

The Conversation Soars

There is a stone bench at a crossroads in the Scottish border country. On the back of the bench are chiseled the words, "Rest and be thankful."

The fourth step of prayer is thanksgiving. It follows confession as morning follows night. Just as praise expresses our love for who God is, thanksgiving is an irrepressible response for what He has done. And when we know we are forgiven, our thanksgiving soars to God for the greatest revelation of His grace, the giving of His Son to suffer and die for our sins. We want to exclaim with Paul and Christians down through the centuries, "Thanks be to God for His indescribable gift!" (2 Corinthians 9:15).

The Bible never stops reminding us to give thanks. "O give thanks to the Lord" is the constant admonition of psalmist, prophet, and apostle. As Son of Man, Jesus often prayed, "I thank You, Father." Now as our risen, reigning Lord, He leads us in our thanksgiving. From a crucial event in His ministry on earth, we discover how important gratitude is to God, to our spiritual growth, and to the impact of our lives on others. Christ teaches us that God desires it, we require it, and others never tire of it.

God Desires Our Thanksgiving

We learn that God desires our thanksgiving from Christ's encounter with the Samaritan lepers on the road to Jerusalem.

Watch Jesus carefully, listen to Him intently, thoughtfully note His reactions. In Him we behold the face of God, listen to God's heart, and sense God's responses to us.

As Jesus passed through Samaria on His way to face the cross, He was confronted with a band of tenfold misery. Outcasts from society on two counts. Lepers, untouchable by law. Samaritans, half-breeds abhorred by the Jews.

But these lepers knew something about Jesus: He broke down barriers of national prejudice—He spoke to Samaritans, loved them, healed them. All of that, but most of all: He *touched* lepers and healed them!

"Jesus! Master! Have mercy on us!" these Samaritan lepers cried.

Jesus' response seems strange. No laying on of His hand, no immediate healing of the oozing sores on their bodies.

"Go show yourselves to the priests," He said.

The priests were the medical officers. They alone could give a certificate pronouncing the lepers well.

Imagine...those lepers had to turn and take the greatest faith journey of their lives. Faith that by the time they reached the priests they would be healed of their leprosy. Faith that Christ had done it with the power of His word alone. Faith in Him!

On their way to see the priests the lepers suddenly realized they had been healed. Jesus had done it!

Strange twist: Only one returned to thank Jesus. Hard to comprehend, isn't it? Or is it? Think of the blessings we take for granted. Perhaps some of the nine thought they deserved their healing, with all the suffering they had been through; the others may have thought they earned it from God by some mysterious barter system in their souls.

> Blow, blow thou winter wind,
> Thou art not so unkind
> As man's ingratitude...

Only one of the lepers returned to express his gratitude. Look at him run to the Master. His feet would not carry him fast enough. When he reached Jesus, he shouted his thanks to God and threw himself on his face, prostrate at Jesus' feet, thanking Him for healing his disease.

As the leper repeated his "Thank you, Jesus, oh, thank you, thank you, thank you," Jesus remained silent. He looked around and then to the sky, expressing His own gratitude that He was one with the Father in healing the misery of human suffering. Then, still looking up, His face clouded over. He shared something else with the Father. Humankind's ingratitude.

"Were there not ten cleansed? But where are the nine?"

More is expressed in that pathos-drenched question than we may have grasped. Would the response to His sacrifice on the cross meet the same ingratitude? We ponder that. How would we answer?

Just before Jesus turned His face again to Jerusalem and the cross, He said to the one grateful leper, "Arise, go your way. Your faith has made you well." Ah, faith, that impelling gift of the Spirit that enables an appreciation and acceptance of what God offers in Christ!

As we reflect on what we have witnessed, suddenly a captivating thought grips us: It meant a great deal to Jesus that the grateful leper returned to give thanks. We are stunned by the moving realization that He desired gratitude. And remember, He is Immanuel, "God with us." From Him we learn what God requires and desires. If the thanks of a cleansed leper could bring joy to the travel-weary bearer of the sins of the world, then we know that our gratitude can fill a special place in God's heart reserved for each of us and our thanks.

But the living Christ knows us today. He knows our fickle hearts. So often we are like the nine; we run off with His blessings as if we had them coming to us. Yet now He doesn't let us run far. He catches us and helps us give thanks to God. He realizes that gratitude is the memory of the heart. He doesn't want us to forget. He won't let us forget!

> Bless the LORD, O my soul,
> and forget not all His benefits (Psalm 103:2).

Just think of it! There is something we can do for God. Saying, "Thank You," in our prayers gives Him delight. Can we, will we, let go and pour forth our thanks? But even here He must help us. And so we pray, "You have given so much; give me one more gift: a thankful heart."

Thankfulness is not an option. Paul tells us it is a vital aspect of God's will for us.

> In everything give thanks; for this is the will of God in Christ Jesus for you (1 Thessalonians 5:18).

We all want to know and do God's will. I get more inquiries about how to know God's will than any other question. People want to know God's plan for their lives. Thanksgiving is one thing that applies to everyone; it's a need we all share. Thanksgiving is a necessary attitude to release our faith. The attitude of gratitude increases the aptitude of faith. The two go together. That's why giving thanks is part of the will of God for us. He loves us and desires His best for our lives.

Want to know more of the will of God for your life? Start thanking Him for all He's done for you. Andrew Murray said, "To be thankful for what I have received, and for what my Lord has prepared, is the surest way to receive more." Thankfulness realizes and acknowledges God's blessings; it prepares us to receive more of what God has to give; it is the antidote to difficulty and despair. That's why God desires gratitude. But further...

We Require Gratitude

Gratitude is required of us because it breaks the bond of our dogged insistence that we are self-sufficient. True gratitude is one of the most mature, advanced, and difficult expressions of the human heart! It requires the recognition that we are not in control, that life and our talents are gifts given to us: that what we have, and what we have become, are evidences of God's providential care.

Cicero said, "A thankful heart is not only the greatest virtue, but the parent of all other virtues." If so, then humility is its first offspring. John Henry Jowett said, "Every virtue divorced from thankfulness is maimed and limps along the spiritual road." But if thankfulness and humility are our legs, we can run the race of life with a runner's high. And as we run, the psalmist cheers, "O, give thanks to the LORD, for He is good" (Psalm 107:1).

Paul's questions to the Corinthians focus our need for gratitude and humility:

> What do you have that you did not receive? Now if you did indeed receive it, why do you boast as if you had not received it? (1 Corinthians 4:7).

The apostle presses the issue. We have received everything: It was all given to us, but the desire to take credit—grab the glory—is our human proclivity. That's why gratitude is one course in the School of Life from which we will never graduate. With our heart dilated by the cross, there's always reason for thanksgiving.

Sin is basically ingratitude. It causes us to love things and use people as if they belonged to us and were under our control. We think we can do what we want, how we want, with no accountability.

The opposite is a sense of the sacredness of everything and every person. Moses commanded the people of Israel, "So you shall rejoice in every good thing which the LORD your God has given to you" (Deuteronomy 26:11). When we rejoice in what we have and the people entrusted to us, our attitude changes, and what we should or should not do with God's sacred gifts is radically transformed. Robert Louis Stevenson caught that view of life: "Everything's grace—we walk upon it, we breath it, we live and die by it, it makes the nails and axles of the universe."

Joyce Kilmer's famous line, "Thank God for God," gets us back to the essence of the attitude of gratitude. Thank Him for His goodness, faithfulness, and unchanging love. The step of thanksgiving in our conversation with God helps us with our problems. We can't really trust God with our difficulties until we can thank Him for allowing them, and for how He will use them for our good and the solution for His glory. You probably sensed that I worded what I just said very carefully. You're right! God doesn't send problems. He doesn't have to, there are enough to go around from people themselves and the force of evil. But God can use whatever occurs to help us trust Him more and give us further evidence that He can bring good out of evil.

Someone said an atheist's most embarrassing moment is when he feels profoundly thankful for something but can't think of anyone to thank for it. Christina Rossetti reflected on that: "Imagine being in this world with grateful hearts—and no one to thank." Both comments, however, are fanciful rhetoric.

In the Bible, a thankful heart and giving thanks is a direct human response inspired by what God has done. It is never vague appreciation, but very specific gratitude induced by God's Spirit. This is especially true in the New Testament where the miracle of the cross, the resurrection, and the power of the risen, present Spirit of Christ, kept the women and men of the early church in constant thanksgiving.

Do you see where this has led us in our thinking? We've come to it again, as in all the steps of prayer: It is the Lord who guides the conversation and He calls us to thanksgiving because He knows we need to humbly recognize our dependence. And then He multiplies our gratitude by bringing to mind all for which we need to be thankful—including all of our difficulties and demanding challenges that are actually potential blessings wrapped up in what look like problems.

Conversation of Thanksgiving

The conversation of thanksgiving begins by the Lord encouraging us to begin to express our gratitude. It isn't long before He adds, "And have you thought of this?" A free-flowing exchange creates such joy in spontaneously moving from one thanks to another.

So often when I converse with the Lord in the thanksgiving step of prayer, He brings people to mind and encourages me to thank Him for them. Sometimes that's a stretch. As well as reminding me to express thanks for some people I might have missed on my gratitude list, He also suggests some others for whom I'm not naturally inclined to feel thankful.

But the change that takes place in my attitude toward these people is amazing! Often this prayer of thanksgiving is prompted by the Lord because He knows (but I don't) of dealings I will have with these people in the future, and He wants me to be prepared. When those encounters occur I'm astounded by how different I suddenly feel, and...surprise!...telling these people I'm thankful for them changes the relationship—that's the relational secret our Lord wants us to discover about gratitude.

People Never Tire of Gratitude

God desires it; we require it; people never tire of it. When our gratitude is guided by the Lord, and we think of people as His gift to us, then genuine gratitude can flow through us to them. It is lifted way beyond manipulation or human relations techniques. There's a great difference between, "Appreciate what you did for me," (which is fine for openers) and "Thanks for being you!" With some people the latter can be said only after the Lord has shown us both the needs and potential of a person. His Spirit warms our hearts with a special love and affirmation for a person. We become delighted with him or her and experience genuine pleasure and enjoyment in our relationship with each individual.

Most of us are stingy affirmers. We feel people will take advantage of us or will think we have condoned their behavior problems and personality quirks. Often, we think we have to keep the pressure on by withholding our encouragement expressed by gratitude for them. Not so! We know from experience that love from people who know our problems gives us courage to change and grow.

However, the greatest cause of our lack of expressed gratitude for people is just plain neglect. We do get busy and become enveloped in our own concerns. But I suspect there's a deeper reason. We probably have not taken very much time in our prayers for thanksgiving. When we do, He not only guides our gratitude for people, but motivates us with specific directions for how to express it to them. You see, He knows when people need encouragement. We should not be surprised when people respond, "Hey, I really appreciated what you said. I needed that. How did you know?"

We'll be talking a lot about how to pray for people in chapter 7, but right now experiment with thanking the Lord for them and then generously expressing our gratitude to them as His gifts to us.

⊱——⊰⊱◈⊰⊱——⊰

Gratitude is also the dominant motive of our ministry in the needs of our society. Our Lord calls us to become involved with the poor, the disadvantaged, and to battle for social justice. No Christian should be AWOL from active involvement in at least one of the crises or areas of human suffering in his or her community. We can never forget what God has done for us in Christ, so what we do should be rooted in gratitude. We'll soon wear ourselves out in "do-goodism" if gratitude isn't our primary motivation.

Prayers of gratitude, renewed every day and motivated by the cross, will keep us going. We can be generous in giving our time, money, and energy when fueled by the realization of how much we have been loved.

We have come full circle. Grace instigates gratitude, and gratitude inspires generosity.

6

Conversation
in
Silence

One day years ago, when I was carrying on a conversation of prayer with God, an amazing thing happened after I finished the steps of preparation, praise, confession, and thanksgiving.

Just as I was about to press on with prayers for others and myself, I turned to Isaiah to listen to the Lord call me into the next step of prayer. My glance fell on Isaiah 41:1. It was a word from the Lord I needed to hear:

> Keep silence before Me, O coastlands,
> And let the people renew their strength!
> Let them come near; *then* let them speak.

The Lord seemed to be saying, "Lloyd, be silent now for a while. Then you will be able to pray for the needs of others and for your own with greater clarity. Your words are like the restless lapping of the sea on the coastlands. Just be still and listen." I felt like Elijah being told to listen for the still, small voice. Only what came in the silence was anything but still or small! When God speaks through the thoughts of our minds in *our* silence, His voice is resounding.

Creative Solitude

That requires creative solitude...times alone with God when we can discover who we really are and be completely honest with ourselves and God.

A tourist to Hollywood saw Robert Redford on an elevator. "Are you the real Robert Redford?" she asked in star-struck amazement. "Only when I'm alone," the famous movie actor replied.

Carl Sandburg used to say, "One of the greatest necessities in America is to discover creative solitude. I go out there and walk and look at the trees and sky. I listen to the sounds of loneliness. I sit on a rock or stump and say to myself, 'Who are you, Sandburg? Where have you been and where are you going?'"

Instead of listening to the sounds of loneliness, we listen to what God has to say. What Samuel Johnson said about human conversations is not true of our conversation with God in prayer. He said, "Silence propagates itself, and the longer talk has been suspended the more difficult it is to find anything to say." Not so with God. Our silence in which He speaks to us gives us the things to say in the next stages of prayer. Intercession and supplication become much more specific with what God wants us to ask, and what He desires to answer.

Edward Gibbon said, "I am never less alone than when I am with myself." I'd say, "I'm never less alone than when I am alone with God."

But being silent is not easy in the welter of words in our culture. Movie producer Samuel Goldwyn was famous for his quick quips as well as movie-making. One day after an uncustomary period of being quiet, he said, "I'm exhausted from not talking!"

And we can imagine that there was a tongue in George Bernard Shaw's cheek when he said, "I believe in the discipline of silence, and could talk for hours about it."

But silence is not creative simply because we're not talking. George Eliot said, "It is ridiculous to suppose that silence is always brooding on a nest full of eggs."

However, we don't have to suppose; we can know, indeed, that silence in conversation with God is the most creative brooding. Of course, it's not to hatch our own eggs, but to allow God to hatch His ideas in our thinking as preparation for our further praying.

There's a "dialectic of silence," to use Arnold Toynbee's words. It's a withdrawal and return. In prayer, it's a withdrawal from talking to God so we can listen to Him and then return to our petitions for others and ourselves with greater clarity.

Michelangelo used to have long pauses between blows on his sculptor's chisel. "Why?" asked a friend. "I can make the decisive move only after being silent," was the reply. It's no less true for our prayers!

Thomas Moore wrote these words in his poem "As Down in the Sunless Retreats":

> As down in the sunless retreats of the Ocean
> Sweet flowers are springing no mortal can see,
> So deep in my soul the still prayer of devotion,
> Unheard by the world, rises silent to Thee.

The Purpose of Silence

The purpose of silence is to receive the wisdom to pray for others and ourselves. We claim the promise from James 1:5:

> If any of you lacks wisdom, let him ask of God, who gives to all liberally and without reproach, and it will be given him.

Our response is a personal wording of Proverbs 3:5-6:

> I will trust in the Lord with all my heart, and lean not on my own understanding; in all my ways, I will acknowledge Him, and He shall direct my paths.

In silence we live out the wise advice of the psalmist, "Wait on the Lord; be of good courage, and He shall strengthen your heart; wait, I say, on the Lord!" (Psalm 27:14). To wait on the Lord is to listen to Him. In the quiet He will form in our minds what is the maximum prayer for others and ourselves. When we unfold what's on our minds, He will speak through the Scriptures, our thoughts, and our inner feelings. When we honestly pray, "Lord, help me to ask for what You want to give," He answers. The psalmist had that assurance, "The meditation of my heart shall give understanding" (Psalm 49:3).

In the process of silent meditation, the most complicated problems yield to solutions. We are given wisdom and insight we could not achieve by ourselves. The wonder of it all! That the Creator and Sustainer of the universe is able and more than willing to inspire our thoughts so we can know what to pray.

The Purification of Our Petitions

In silence our petitions are purified. We come to this stage of prayer with our hopes and desires like excavated silver ore that must be smelted in the fires of God's righteousness. It is the particular ministry of the reigning Christ. Malachi predicted how the Messiah would oversee the purification of God's people. It is when we are silent that petitioner and petition get cleansed of the dross of selfishness, self-aggrandizement, and efforts to run our own or others' lives.

> For He is like a refiner's fire
> And like launderers' soap.
> He will sit as a refiner and a purifier of silver;
> He will purify the sons of Levi,
> And purge them as gold and silver,
> That they may offer to the LORD
> An offering in righteousness (Malachi 3:2-3).

The images of this challenging promise are fascinating. Understanding them greatly enhances what Christ wants to do in our silence to prepare our petitions for presentation to the Father.

When silver was excavated it was mixed in with dirt and gravel. These impurities had to be sifted out. Then the unrefined silver was placed in a large crucible over a very hot fire, bellowed into white-hot heat. The dross would rise to the top and be skimmed off by the refiner. He would sit by the crucible watching. He knew that the silver was purged when he could look into the crucible and see his own face. Then the molten silver was poured into molds to cool.

When the ingots were formed, they were ready for the refiner's file and polishing.

When we are silent, I think the same thing happens to us and to the petitions we want to present in our prayers of intercession and supplication. We sit alone. Our minds are filled with requests we want to make. They are like raw silver ore excavated out of a side of a mountain. We can't see the value of the silver because of all the earth and gravel around and the impurities in it. But we know it's there.

First, comes the sifting process to separate the silver ore from the gravel and dirt. Willfullness, pride, and our cravings for control are always mixed in with the honest concerns. These have to be separated from the raw silver of a petition.

Then, even after the sifting, the silver or gold is not yet purified. It still has to be placed in the Lord's crucible to purge it of the impure minerals of our wish-dreams for others and ourselves. This dross bubbles to the surface, and the thick layers of it must then be skimmed off by our Lord. This is disturbing. We recognize much of our own self-serving egos in our petitions.

But the Lord continues. He sits by the crucible, waiting, skimming, watching. When the silver of our soul is ready, He does exactly what the refiner of metals does: He pours out our purified desires, forms them in the mold of His will for us, files and polishes them, and then presents them as refined requests to the Father. "He always lives to make intercession for [us]" (Hebrews 7:25).

All this happens while we are silent. To dare to be alone with God requires courage. Sometimes we would rather bluster on to the next step of prayer without the silence that refines our petitions. But the Lord wants to see His face in the crucible. He wants to be sure the impurities of our requests have risen to the surface and have been removed by Him.

What follows is not easy: to feel the file of the Lord taking off the rough edges! And yet, if we are to accept the high calling of being intercessors and bold supplicants, it is required.

Note in this Malachi passage, that it is the sons of Levi who were to be purified. Good reason. They were the caretakers of the Ark of the Covenant and later the temple. (After the tablets of the Ten Commandments were given to Moses, they were placed in a large wooden chest, or box, covered with gold and carvings, called the Ark of the Covenant. It symbolized the presence of Yahweh with His people.) When the people moved in the wilderness, the sacred task of carrying the Ark was performed by the sons of Levi. They also set up and arranged the tabernacle and did all the preparation for worship. After the temple was built in Jerusalem, the Levites became the caretakers of the sanctuary and assisted the priests in leading worship.

In a sense, we are contemporary Levites. We carry the ark of God's commandments, the gospel of His son, the treasure of our biblical faith. Our hearts are a sanctuary, too; offerings there must be made with purified prayers and refined petitions.

It is very significant that after the purifying of the sons of Levi predicted by Malachi, they would then be the ones to offer to the Lord an offering in righteousness.

Neither can we make an offering to the Lord in righteousness until the Lord does His purifying and refining. Our petitions and supplications must be right, in keeping with God's own character. And since we have no righteousness on our own, they must be prayed in Christ's name, for He alone is our righteousness.

Through Christ and the cross, we have become the righteousness of God. It is an awesome status. We have access to God through Christ, but Christ through the Holy Spirit helps us to be what we are. This is especially true as He takes us at whatever stage of growth we are and continues to purify and reform us, and the prayers we pray.

The Challenges of Silence

Allow me to empathize with how you may be thinking and feeling at this point. I sense that you are anxious to get on to making your requests in prayers of intercession and supplication. And here I am slowing up the process by suggesting that you be silent for a time before you do what most of us think is prayer: telling God what we, and those we care about, need.

My recommendation for silence at this stage of our conversation in prayer is motivated by the difference it has made in my own prayers ever since that day when God stopped me in my tracks, just before intercession and supplication.

I'd learned about the benefits of silence on spiritual retreats and during my solitary weeks of study leave each summer, but had not applied them on a daily basis. In those prolonged periods of silence I was always alarmed by what I discovered about myself and my need to grow. I realized how shallow were my prayers for loved ones, friends, the church, and my expectations for the results of my work. I lived in a constricted cubicle of vision! The Lord then blew off the top and knocked down the walls. I saw the immense potential of what He wanted in me, people, and situations.

After those periodic times of silence, I would drift back into all-talk prayer. Even when claiming Scripture promises I was still only making sounds. Then the Lord told me to be silent right in the middle of my prayers for that day. I knew He was not telling me to take some days off for a silent retreat. Instead, right there, that moment, I was to be silent.

So I obeyed. The results were stunning. Exactly that! I was stunned by what thoughts He placed in my mind and the way He refined the petitions I was about to rush on to make. That day I resolved to make silence a vital part of my daily prayers.

There's nothing to be lost and everything to be gained by trying at least five minutes of your daily prayer time in absolute silence. Place your open hands on your lap, symbolic of your willingness to receive. Begin the silence by simply telling God that you are willing to have the Refiner probe and purge, refine and polish you as a person and the subsequent requests you will make. And then wait on the Lord!

When Thoughts Wander

Don't worry if your mind wanders. When this happens you have probably wandered to something that needs to be revealed. Our minds often drift off to problems or people about which we are concerned. Sometimes old memories surface, or deep tears well up and flow. These thoughts are a part of who you are and the Lord takes you seriously. Allow each thought to play out and then listen for what the Lord has to say about it.

Sometimes I'm tempted to say, "Lloyd, get your mind back on God!" But when the thought persists, I know the Lord has something to say about it, or the deeper problem at the lower levels of my subconscious mind. The same is true of wild fantasies that pop up. Why did I think of that when I am supposed to be concentrating on the Lord? And yet in that fantasy there are hidden desires the Lord must refine or diffuse.

Someone Doesn't Want You to Be Silent

Satan abhors our silent prayers. He knows that they put us in direct contact with the Lord. So he will use all sorts of tactics to keep us from it. He will try to convince us we don't have time; he will arrange perturbing interruptions; he will try to ridicule us for thinking we can receive direct communication from the Lord *(What are you pretending to be—some monk in a monastery or some super-saint?)*; he tries to make us impatient with our first attempts so we won't try it again. Sometimes he tries to influence us with thoughts of our unworthiness for such uplifting times of silence. And there are times when he is the author of aberrant thoughts that blast our concentration.

I had one of these times in my morning silence recently. When I began, my mind dramatized for me all sorts of negative thoughts about people and situations. I was utterly amazed at how bad I thought things were going to turn out. Now that's not my nature— especially after being born again—and so I knew that I was being hassled by Ol' Scratch. "I belong to Christ," I said. "Now take your hands off of His property!" Then in my silence I could listen up—to the Lord—and brighten up about what lay ahead of me that day.

In the next chapters we will be talking a lot about how the imagination is used in formulating our petitions. We get ready for that in this strategic step of silence.

For now, enjoy the Lord in silence. Nothing will do more to relax our tensions, quiet our nerves, unwind the tightly wound spring of stress inside us. And there's no other way for the refiner to purify us and what we will ask.

Listen to God before you ask Him to listen to your requests!

7

Conversation
About
People

Most everyone likes to talk about people. Ever notice how much time we spend in our daily conversations talking, analyzing, criticizing, gossiping about people? They fascinate and frustrate us. And we vent both feelings by endless talk. Family members, friends, people at work, our neighbors, celebrities, spiritual, and political leaders. The famous and the infamous get top billing in our conversations.

Recently in Birmingham, England, a street corner newspaper was hawking a headline about some escapade of a member of the royal family. I overheard a woman say to her husband, "Don't know what we'd have to talk about if the Queen's family didn't give us juicy bits to clack over." The husband replied, "You'd find something, Luv!"

In America, the personal and public lives of people in Washington or Hollywood are the target for our quarterback-analysis or our armchair "pop" psychology. Millions of "rag sheets" sold every day supply a steady flow of material for our conversations.

Christians spend a great deal of time talking over their concerns about the problems and failures of other believers. A lot of "concerned" gossip sometimes precedes asking people to pray for others. And it sounds so sympathetic and caring.

If only we spent as much time talking to God about people as we spend talking to others about people! Nothing helps us to love people more than praying about and for them.

The H.O.I.

You and I have been called to be members of the Holy Order of Intercessors. The Lord now presses us on in our conversation with Him to learn how to exercise our responsibilities as part of this royal priesthood. The next stage of conversation with God is intercession.

The word *intercession* means to approach another person on behalf of someone else. Interceding in our conversation with God is approaching Him on behalf of others. He introduces the subject, reminds us of our privileges and authority, and also helps us know how and what to pray. We are priests of God through our Lord Jesus Christ and are guided by the Holy Spirit in our priestly prayers.

The word *priest* may startle you. It shouldn't. A priest is one who goes to God for another and brings from God His blessings for another. To be in Christ is to be in the H.O.I. The question is how well we are exercising our calling. A credit card company has the slogan, "Membership has its privileges." Membership in the H.O.I. has the privilege of being part of what God wants to do in the lives of people.

Presuppositions for Intercessors

There are some basic presuppositions that undergird our calling as intercessors.

God our Father is constantly seeking to bring us, His children, together in His love.

He is delighted when we come to Him out of love for our sisters and brothers.

Often, He waits to bless the people of our lives until we intercede for them.

Intercession changes our understanding of what and how to pray, changes our relationships with the people for whom we pray, and actually changes what happens in their lives because we prayed.

Prayers for people are to be made in Jesus' name and are guided by the Holy Spirit.

As priests of the Lord, we have authority to go to Him about people and bring His assurance and courage to them. Listen to Christ's promise:

> Most assuredly, I say to you, he who believes in Me, the works that I do he will do also; and greater works than these he will do, because I go to My Father. And whatever you ask in My name, that I will do, that the Father may be glorified in the Son. If you ask anything in My name, I will do it. If you love Me, keep My commandments (John 14:12-15).

This promise was given on the night before the crucifixion. Jesus anticipated the glorious victory of the cross and resurrection. He looked forward to the time He would baptize His followers with the Holy Spirit (Acts 2:32-33) and as reconciled, redeemed people they would be able to pray for others in His name. The "greater work" they would be able to do would be to pray for people to know and trust Him as risen, victorious, Savior and Lord, and the work would expand in the adventure of introducing them to Him.

All our prayers of intercession revolve around people's greatest need to meet Christ, grow in Him, and face life's challenges and opportunities with His power. Hebrews 7:25 shows us the way:

> Therefore He is able to save to the uttermost those who come to God through Him, since He always lives to make intercession for them.

Christ, Our Example

During His ministry on earth, Christ exemplified intercessory prayer. He prayed for His disciples all through those three years. They were on His heart in those times when He slipped away to be alone with the Father.

A specific example is Christ's prayer for Peter's vacillation.

> Simon, Simon! Indeed, Satan has asked for you, that he may sift you as wheat. *But I have prayed for you,* that your faith should not fail; and when you have returned to Me, strengthen your brethren (Luke 22:31-32).

In Christ's prayer that night for all of the disciples, recorded for us in John 17, we listen in on Christ's intercessory prayers. He prayed that the disciples would be one with one another, with Him and with the Father. Also, He prayed for their strength to overcome Satan's influence. And that they would grow in holiness. In Luke 18:1, Christ gave us the motto for intercessory prayer, that we "always ought to pray and not lose heart."

One of the most liberating discoveries I've made about intercessory prayer over the years is that my task is to listen in on Christ's intercession. I ask, "What would He pray for the people on my heart?" He reveals that through the Holy Spirit. Then I can pray with both authority and confidence. I am given discernment way beyond my own analysis.

For Whom Should We Pray?

Under the inspiration of the Holy Spirit, the apostle Paul gave us the chapter for the Holy Order of Intercessors. What he wrote to Timothy became our guide.

> Therefore I exhort first of all that supplications, prayers, intercessions, and giving thanks be made for all men, for kings and all who are in authority, that we may lead a quiet and peaceable life in all godliness and reverence. For this is good and acceptable in the sight of God our Savior, who desires all men to be saved and come to the knowledge of the truth. For there is one God and one Mediator between God and men, the Man Christ Jesus, who gave Himself a ransom for all....I desire that men pray everywhere, lifting up holy hands, without wrath and doubting (1 Timothy 2:1-6,8).

So the answer to the question, for whom should we intercede, is first, everyone; then people in authority and those who lead. In the "everyone" category are loved ones, family, friends, neighbors, and people with whom we work. That makes a long list!

The place to start is with our inner circle of people: our family members and friends. The Holy Spirit puts on our hearts those whom He has placed on our personal agenda. These are people we are led to pray for as well as those who ask us to pray for them. It's a sacred trust for those of us in the H.O.I., so never say, "I'll pray for you," unless you mean it and intend to follow through.

Next on the agenda are leaders. I begin with the president and vice president, then the governor of my state, and then the mayor of my city, and local officials. This is basic to the sacred responsibility of citizenship. (Those reading this in other countries may simply shift the titles of government officials.) Praying for those in civil authority does not mean that we must agree with their political philosophy, programs, or actions. Nor does it mean that because we pray for them we never oppose them or become involved in political action as guided by God and the Scriptures. Our first and ultimate loyalty is to God and His kingdom above any nation, political party, or leader.

The leadership of the church is also a focus for our daily intercession. The pastor and lay leaders of the local church, along with denominational officials, urgently need our prayers. The program of the local church and the movement of Christianity in the world is dependent on biblically rooted, Christ-centered, Holy Spirit–filled leaders. I, for one, know that I could not do what I am called to do without the prayers of my people. Put your pastor and the lay officers of your congregation high on your intercessory prayer list. Your fondest hopes for your local church will never be reached without consistent intercessory prayer.

Missionaries are also urgently in need of our prayers. In my congregation we publish a list of our missionaries and those involved in special ministries so that we can pray for several each day. Paul consistently reminded the churches that he was praying for them; he also constantly asked for their prayers.

Next, I feel called to pray for the sick and those who are facing physical, emotional, and relational problems. James tells us that the "prayer of faith will save the sick, and the Lord will raise him up" (James 5:15). How the Lord chooses to do that must be surrendered to Him. Our calling is to pray for healing in Christ's name; how that healing is performed is up to the Lord. Our responsibility is to pray boldly and to leave the results and the timing up to Him. Years of praying for the sick convinces me that God answers these prayers. I've seen miracles of physical and psychological healing. But I'm no less impressed when God gives a person strength to endure an illness when healing is delayed.

Guidelines for Intercessory Prayer

There are at least four clear guidelines for intercessory prayer. These have been of immeasurable help to me as I have tried to be an attentive student and disciple in the school of prayer.

1. Pray intelligently. That means listening intently to what people say, and hear what is being expressed beneath the level of words. The Holy Spirit gives us the gift of discernment to know what the Lord is seeking to do in a person's life and also helps us see when he or she is being hassled by the forces of evil. When we ask for guidance on how to pray before we intercede, often profound insight is given to us to pray more intelligently.

2. Pray imaginatively. Closely related to the first guideline, this one employs our imagination when it is committed to the Lord. The Spirit helps us to picture the person we're praying for as whole, secure, healed. With that picture focused, we can pray with greater conviction and courage.

3. Pray powerfully. Remember that every prayer in the name of Christ is empowered by Him. Through the Spirit we are guided to pray whatever He's praying in His intercession for a person. Sometimes we just don't know what that is and so must depend on the Holy Spirit who knows our love and our concern, but also knows the Lord's greater strategy for a person.

Likewise the Spirit also helps us in our weaknesses. For we do not know what we should pray for as we ought, but the Spirit Himself makes intercession for us with groanings which cannot be uttered. Now He who searches the hearts knows what the mind of the Spirit is, because He makes intercession for the saints according to the will of God (Romans 8:25-26).

So our prayer is, "Holy Spirit, take my intercession, reword it, purify it, and wing it straight to the heart of our eternal Intercessor who is constantly interceding for us." The Father, Son and Holy Spirit are working in close harmony, to bring about the Father's will for those for whom we pray. Trust the Holy Spirit to interpret your prayers to be in keeping with the Divine plan.

4. *Pray constantly.* Paul called the Thessalonians to "pray without ceasing" (1 Thessalonians 5:17), told Timothy that he prayed for him without ceasing (2 Timothy 1:3), assured the Christians at Rome that he made mention of them in his prayers without ceasing (Romans 1:9). This means that in addition to a consistent time of intercessory prayer in our daily time alone with the Lord, we are called to be intercessors all through the day. Brief arrows of prayer can be sent off when we observe needs, talk with people, or are asked to pray for them. Often when we are busy doing something else, our minds suddenly focus on a person. That's a call for intercessory prayer.

The other day, a man's face was repeatedly focused in my mind's eye. After the sixth time, I called him. "Is there some reason you've been on my mind today with an urgent signal to pray?" I asked. "Sure is!" he replied, "It's been one of the toughest days I've had in years." He related the problem and we prayed together on the phone.

Being an Effective Intercessor

Effective intercessors are also readily receptive to others' prayers for them. It's heartening to note how often Paul asked for intercessory prayer. He was able to receive as well as give.

> Now I beg you, brethren, through the Lord Jesus Christ, and through the love of the Spirit, that you strive together with me in prayers to God for me (Romans 15:30).

Asking others to pray for us makes us a vulnerable prayer partner, rather than coming across as one who has God's ear but has no needs of his own. We all need a trusted circle of friends with whom we can confide and know that we will be interceded for with faith and boldness. And the evidence of the results of those prayers increases our own confidence in the power of intercessory prayer.

Confidentiality

People trust confidential intercessors. They need to know that what they ask us to pray for will go directly to the Lord in prayer and to no one else. We simply don't trust people to pray for us if they've talked about and told us what they've been asked to pray for by someone else. This may sharply limit our conversations about people. If we are a person's intercessor and also talk about them to others, the flow of power stops and our trust from others is debilitated.

The Prayer Diary

A private intercessory prayer log is very important in order to list people and their needs and the results of our prayers. This kind of journaling keeps our memories clear and helps us rejoice over the results that follow, glorifying God with those for whom we have been praying.

There should be a space for the person's name, the need prayed for, and the subsequent progress in the person's life. Another important item to note is what we've done to communicate to the person that we have prayed. A brief letter or phone call means a great deal to people. There are few things worse than for people to ask us to pray, and then, when we see them again, not ask them how things are going and assure them of our prayers. A request for intercessory prayer is a sacred trust and people need to know we have taken them seriously.

Every so often it's good to take an inventory of our response to the awesome calling to be an intercessor. How would you answer these searching questions:

- Have I spent as much time talking to God about people as I have spent talking to others about them?

- Do I really believe that God has ordained intercessory prayer as a way for us to share in His care of people and that He waits to give some of His blessings until we pray?

- Are we willing to go about our calling as intercessors in an orderly way so that we can really follow through when we say we will pray for people?

If you have said "Yes" to these questions, you are a member of the H.O.I.—the Holy Order of Intercessors!

8

Conversation About Peace

In each of the steps of prayer as conversation, we have utilized Scripture to listen to God and have personalized great verses in the first person to make our response.

After we have interceded for the needs of others, the Lord encourages us to get in touch with what's on our own minds about ourselves and our lives. He loves each of us as if there were only one of us. And He's deeply concerned about the worries that rob us of peace. His peace. The peace Christ offers.

> Peace I leave with you, My peace I give to you; not as the world gives do I give to you. Let not your heart be troubled, neither let it be afraid (John 14:27).

Our response, worded personally, can be, "I will be anxious for nothing, but in everything by prayer and supplication, with thanksgiving, I will let my requests be made known to God; and the peace of God, which surpasses all understanding, will guide my heart and mind through Christ Jesus" (see Philippians 4:6-7).

The next step of conversation with God is supplication. The word has a formal, lofty ring. Actually, it represents a very down-to-earth, personal kind of prayer. The Greek word is *deesis* and means the expression of wanting, needing, and asking, with heartfelt entreaty. The word stresses a sense of need.

Well, the one thing we all have is need. Anything that can deny us of the peace that Christ promised us, and died to establish with us, is worthy of our supplications. The peace Christ offers us is not the peace of lethargic ennui, or a sheltered life, or stoic emotionlessness. His peace is for disciples in the midst of the battle.

William Gladstone, at the height of conflict and discord around him, shared the secret of his calm. "At the foot of my bed, where I can see it on retiring, and the first thing on rising, are these words, 'You will keep him in perfect peace, whose mind is stayed on You, because he trusts in You'" (Isaiah 26:3).

As someone aptly put it, "When at night you cannot sleep, talk to the Shepherd and stop counting sheep."

Edwin Markham expressed the repose of a heart set in God's peace:

> At the heart of the cyclone tearing the sky,
> And flinging the clouds and flowers on,
> Is a place of central calm;
> And so in the roar of mortal things,
> There's a place where my spirit sings,
> In the hollow of God's palm.

That reminds us of the promised security of God's hands. "I will not forget you. See, I have inscribed you on the palms of My hands" (Isaiah 49:15-16). With confidence we can pray the ancient Hebrew childhood prayer repeated by Jesus on the cross, "Father, into Your hands I commit my spirit" (see Psalm 31:5). It is in supplication that we get ourselves "off" of our own hands and into the hands of God.

But how do we do that with the jumbled mass of anxieties we all feel most of the time? We can take them one by one and talk to our Father about them until we reach the peace inside that He offers us in Christ. Quite apart from our concerns for others that we already have entrusted to Him, He is ready to hear whatever we are feeling about our own problems, perceived insecurities, and inadequacies.

Jesus' repeated response to the cries for help from people was, "What do you want Me to do for you?" Well, how would you answer for today? He already knows, but He also understands that there is a therapeutic release when we can talk them out in honest supplication.

Conquest of Anxieties

Paul's admonition to be anxious for nothing seems impossible to fulfill. That's why in the same breath the apostle gives the way to do it. His prescription for anxiety includes "everything." Whatever is big enough to trouble us is worthy of supplication. Supplication is God's way of helping us with a fearful imagination. We focus these fears and He reforms the picture of ourselves by showing us what He will be able to be and do through us. Paul's admonition to have no anxiety must always be considered along with his confession of confidence, not in himself, but in Christ. "I can do all things through Christ who strengthens me" (Philippians 4:13). The apostle was using his imagination to picture what Christ could do, rather than what he knew he was unable to do on his own.

Many of us are dominated by "negative imagination." Our peace of mind is invaded by frightening thoughts. Fearful possibilities are portrayed on the picture screen of our minds. The worst that could happen in the problems we face is dramatized in vivid detail. Often, we actually play out the scenario of our failure in some challenge before us. Our concerns about people with whom we feel competitive, or who threaten us, are played out in scenes of discord in which these people play leading roles as antagonists. All this takes place in the inner world of imagination. A God-given faculty of the cerebral cortex, our brains, is misused to exacerbate our deepest fears.

Any serious conquest of these anxieties must eventually confront the tendency of the imagination to produce illusionary fears or greatly expand our panic over those that may have some foundation in reality. As I have said often in my writings, "An imaginary fear may be unreal, but a fearful imagination is very real!"*

---

* Lloyd Ogilvie, *Twelve Steps to Living Without Fear* (Waco, TX: Word, Inc., 1990).

...rson was right:

> Some of your fears you have cured
> And the sharpest you still have survived,
> But what torment of grief you've endured
> From hurts that never arrived.

As I talk with people they often share their "imaginary fears." Some of these fears are rooted in previous experiences. Most people, however, confide that they are particularly adept at exploding their fears way beyond reality by imagining dreadful things that might happen. Afterward, so often people share, "I don't know why I was so anxious; things turned out so much better than I expected."

Active imagining of the worst that can happen often makes us participants in making it happen. Inadvertently, we unconsciously act or react in the way we've pictured ourselves and sometimes bring the reactions of people we expected. The adversary, Satan, is always looking for people he can use to accomplish his clever schemes. That's why daily supplication for God's plan and power is so important: It's a deliberate refusal to cooperate with evil.

Supplication with Thanksgiving

I believe the Holy Spirit inspired Paul to give us the secret of overcoming an anxious imagination. It's a two-step process. We tell the Lord about our needs. We spread them out before Him. That's step one. Thanking Him is step two. How can we thank Him in advance unless we have allowed Him to use our imaginations creatively to picture what would be a resolution for which we could give thanks? If our fearful imaginations can portray the worst, is it not possible for them to be anointed with the Holy Spirit to picture God's best? The issue is: Can we thank the Lord in advance for the result, even if it may mean difficulties in which we are given the opportunity to grow and glorify Him?

Thanksgiving is an ultimate kind of relinquishment. It cannot be expressed without fully trusting the Lord with the results. Repeated daily thanksgiving for a previously made supplication surrenders to God's timing what may seem like unanswered prayer. If we trust God with our supplications, thanksgiving enables us to take delays with patience. And we can accept His denials with the perspective that we wouldn't want something God had deemed less than His best for us anyway. The supplication does not need to be repeated, but the thanksgiving does. Make a request once, then thank the Lord constantly until it is completed.

There are only two ways of living. One is to constantly second-guess God and keep control of our lives; the other, to completely trust Him and give Him control. Supplication with thanksgiving gives Him the control with confident relinquishment.

The promise to us about what happens when we make our supplications with thanksgiving is very exciting:

> The peace of God, which surpasses understanding, will guard your hearts and minds through Christ Jesus (Philippians 4:7).

A Garrison of Peace

Paul uses a military term for the way peace guards our hearts and minds. It is *phrouresei*—the future active indicative of the verb *phroureo*, "To keep by guarding," as a garrison guards a city, protecting it against attack by an enemy. The Philippians to whom Paul wrote this promise would have understood the metaphor. A Roman garrison was stationed in Philippi to guard the outpost colony of the empire.

In the same way we are guarded with the active power of God's shalom, His peace. We are literally surrounded by this peace. It is beyond our capacity to understand by reason alone how Christ Jesus, through the Holy Spirit, gives us security and serenity when things around us jangle with dissonant disturbance and petulant pressure. When we are tempted to think that God has not heard our supplications, we are kept calm if we continue to thank Him for working things out His way on His timing.

Nobody needs that more than I do. As I write this I can think of at least twenty things about which I prayed this morning with supplication and thanksgiving. Some were new supplications, but most of them were requests I had to reaffirm by thanking God for hearing them and for how He is implementing solutions for the ultimate good of all concerned.

Those who know me well, know that patience is not a natural virtue of my personality. And yet, as I sit here alone, I am overcome with a wonderful sense of peace, a calm that is a miracle, a trust that is a gift. I simply do not understand it. However, I should not be surprised: Paul said this kind of peace surpasses understanding. There is every reason, on a human level, that I should be worried, anxious, and impatient. Instead, peace guards my mind and heart—a sublime inner tranquility. And I'm thankful. My prayer is always that I'll remember it the next time my nerves are jangled and my body is agitated by self-endured stress: the results of not making my supplications with the relinquishment of thanksgiving.

My challenge is to claim the guard of peace in the rough and tumble of daily life. I find that's possible only when I consciously reaffirm my surrender of a problem with the supplication I made in my time alone with the Lord. When I get a jab of panic during the day, I pray a brief prayer of thanks: "Father, I gave that over to Your control this morning. Thank You for taking charge of the results. And if there is anything You want me to do to cooperate with what You are doing, please reveal it to me."

Holding the Picture

Above we talked about the negative power of a fearful imagination. Now we need to affirm the positive power of a *Spirit-captivated* imagination. What we claimed in our prayers for others, we now claim in our prayers for ourselves. We saw how important it is for the Holy Spirit to engender a picture of what we are to pray to be accomplished in another's life. The same can happen when we hold the image of ourselves under the Lordship of Christ, manifesting the fruit of the Spirit, really the character of Christ reproduced in us, of love, joy, peace, patience, kindness, goodness, faithfulness, gentleness, and self-control (Galatians 5:22-23). When we make supplication with thanksgiving about our problems and challenges, as well as the opportunities given us, it is liberating to have the Spirit actually project on the screen of our imaginations how we can respond with this spiritual fruit in real-life situations, circumstances, and relationships. We are given the gift of the portrait, and the power to hold it and live it.

◆ ━◆━ ◆

When we pray our supplications with the relinquishment and trust of thanking the Father in advance for His best for our lives, we are usually in for some unexpected surprises. Through the reigning Christ and the inspiration of the Holy Spirit, unanticipated interventions begin happening. People's attitudes change, sticky situations get unstuck, closed doors open, and solutions we could never have dreamed up ourselves begin to surface.

I like to put it this way: Stop making supplications with thanksgiving and the "coincidences" stop happening. The Trinity enjoys working harmoniously to surprise us with grace! Answers to our prayers do not happen by accident. They are arranged by the Lord who was preparing the answer even before we asked!

9

Conversation
About
Guidance

We have been discussing a very personal, intimate relationship with our Father in which He leads us in a conversation of prayer. It is crucial that we do not veer from that dialogue of love and get lost in impersonal rules or theories as we approach the next aspect of prayer.

Once again our Father opens this phase of conversation by assuring us that He will guide us in our decisions and the direction of our lives. He speaks to us in a very colorful, vivid way:

> I will instruct you and teach you in the way you should go; I will guide you with My eye. Do not be like the horse or like the mule, which have no understanding, which must be harnessed with bit and bridle, else they will not come near you (Psalm 32:8-9).

I like these verses as a basis for thinking about the will of God and His guidance because the promise is so clear, and the equestrian simile depicts our human reaction so accurately. Let's allow the impelling progression of thought in these verses to direct our thinking about God's willingness to guide us, how He guides us, and the willingness to be guided that He desires from us.

There is an old Welsh proverb that says, "Three things for which thanks are due: an invitation, a gift, and a warning." The Lord has given us all three in these verses.

The Invitation: To Know God's Will

God created us with a will so that we could will to do His will. He gave us minds to think; emotions to express joy, love, delight; He also gave us wills to decide to do His will for us. Our volitional faculty unites us with the Father. He has a will and He has given us wills. Our supreme purpose is to know and do the will of God.

> To know the will of God is our greatest treasure;
> To do the will of God is our greatest pleasure.

From the beginning God has revealed His will. He created humankind to know, love, and obey Him. To communicate His will He gave us His commandments; He spoke through prophets, priests, and kings to call His people back to obedience to His will; He intervened at times of crisis and challenges to reveal His way and will.

The sad reality, however, is that God's people used the wondrous gift of will, the power of choice, to reject both God's will and His guidance. Let me stress again: We were given free will in order to choose to love and obey Him. He knew there could be no authentic love relationship with us unless we had a choice. He did not make us puppets or marionettes: He wanted us to choose to be chosen, to accept our election to be His people, to delight in the privilege of a relationship with Him. Fundamentally, sin is saying "No!" to Him.

Eventually, God's choice was to either reject humankind or redeem us. He chose redemption. He sent His Son to reveal, in His humanity as Son of Man, what it means for us to do the will of God. It should not be surprising then that Jesus' message was punctuated by constant references to the will of God. "For I have come down from heaven, not to do My own will, but the will of Him who sent Me" (John 6:38). The Master prayed to do the will of God and taught His disciples to pray, "Your will be done on earth as it is in heaven" (Matthew 6:10). And He gave the secret of knowing the will of God, "If anyone wills to do His will, he shall know concerning the doctrine...If you abide in My word, you are My disciples indeed. And you shall know the truth, and the truth shall make you free" (John 7:17; 8:31-32).

But more than an example was required to transform women and men intent on doing their own wills. Rebellious willfulness had to be broken and a new creation begun. As the divine Son of God, Christ went to the cross to suffer for sin (the misuse of the will), and to redeem us, buy us back, transform us from within, to recreate our malignant, volitional faculty. The love and forgiveness, but also the power, of the cross makes us new creatures in Christ.

When we accept Christ as our Savior and Lord we are reconciled to the Father and our wills are liberated by the miracle of grace. Before we wanted only our will. Now, mysteriously, miraculously, there stirs within us a new, dominant desire to know and do God's will. The Holy Spirit is given to us to nurture and mature our volitional faculty so that we can accept the gift of guidance.

The Gift: Guidance in the Will of God

Now we can appreciate so much more than the psalmist did when the Lord said, "I will instruct and teach you the way you should go. I will guide you with My eye."

I had a new awareness of the power of the eye to guide behavior one time when my son, Scott, and his wife, Eileen, brought our three granddaughters over to spend a weekend with my wife, Mary Jane, and me. During a meal before the parents left, I was very impressed by my son's strong discipline and guidance of the children. When they got out of line he would catch their eye and impart a very strong corrective without ever saying a word. He would also give immense affirmation simply by saying one of the girl's names and pouring out encouragement through the look on his face.

I was proud of my son and the quality of his relationship with his children, and briefly entertained the notion that he may have learned all he knew as a father from me. That is, until he and his wife left and I tried the same method on the girls. It didn't work. They know I'm a pushover, and they can melt me with the sound of, "Aww, Papa Lloyd." The reality is that as grandfather, I am not their consistent daily source of discipline and guidance. So when I tried to correct the girls simply by the look in my eye, I did not succeed. But the experience of observing their dad do it clearly demonstrated to me the power of the eye to guide.

My wife is able to guide me with her eye. At a party, she can direct my attention to someone with whom I need to talk. A glance from across the room can speak volumes! And if she's in the audience when I am speaking, her eyes can affirm what I'm saying or tell me that I've made my point and should move on. Sometimes she can tell me that it's time to finish and sit down! I am open to receive the guidance of her eye, because I know she loves me and wants me to do my best for God.

Think of your own experience of being guided by someone's eye. People often say "Yes" or "No" by the look in their eyes. They can also signal danger, or give the go-ahead to what we are saying or doing.

The same is true in a face-to-face relationship with God in the conversation of prayer. In Hebrew, the same word is translated as face and presence.

A sublime moment in Moses' relationship with God came when he opened his heart to Him completely and prayed, "If I have found grace in Your sight, show me now Your way, that I may know You and that I may find grace in Your sight" (Exodus 33:13). The Lord's response to Moses is one of the greatest promises of the Old Testament. People through the ages have staked their lives on it, martyrs have confronted death with it on their lips, and the troubled have grasped it tenaciously as their assurance.

The Lord said to Moses, "My Presence will go with you, and I will give you rest" (verse 14). The Lord's presence! Some translate the word as "face"—the face of the Lord with His watchful eye did not leave Moses and the people. Nor will He ever leave or forsake us. His face is with us.

The face of God was manifested in the incarnate Christ. Now when we seek the face of God we see Christ's face. Follow that face through His ministry on earth. See His eye of indescribable love and forgiveness; observe His eyes as they weep over Jerusalem; behold His eyes flash with holy anger while driving the money changers from the temple. But do not fail to see His eyes on the cross.

Paul never got over seeing the face of God in Christ. Nor can we.

> For it is the God who commanded light to shine out of darkness, who has shone in our hearts to give the light of the knowledge of the glory of God in the face of Jesus Christ (2 Corinthians 4:6).

So it is not by some vague mystical spiritual projection that we see the face and eye of God. He has chosen to guide us through the face of Christ. What Christ has said becomes irrevocable as He catches us with His eye today. He will never contradict His truth by what He guides us to do today.

I have found that the Lord's eye becomes piercingly evident when I seek His guidance. When I ask for guidance for my daily life or my decisions, I find that as I search the Scriptures and then picture His face, I can discern His "Yes," "No," or "Later..." I simply picture His face and read in His eye what He is saying. To be sure, sometimes the thoughts He gives me that communicate His guidance sound in my soul louder than a megaphone shout. But the inner voice of His Spirit never contradicts the look of His eye.

The Lord also uses circumstances to guide us. We must be careful here because adverse circumstances do not always mean that we are headed in the wrong direction. Often it's in these trying circumstances that we are to make our witness for what the Lord can do to strengthen us in difficulties. And the very problems may be the passageway to where the Lord wants us to be. So in prayers for guidance check out circumstances with the Lord as to what He says and the look we discern in His eye.

The inclination of our feelings must go through the same test. Our feelings can vacillate and lead us in the wrong direction. But looking into the Lord's face either encourages or contradicts the inclination of the heart.

When we saturate our minds with daily reading of the Bible, so many questions are answered before we ask them. In the Old Testament we are guided by the words of God; in the New Testament we have the words of Christ. The Lord does not change what He has said to meet our desires; He changes our desires so we want to do what He has said.

Counsel from trusted Christian friends, who have nothing to gain or lose personally by our decisions, can be helpful. The danger is that even the best-meaning friends can project their wills onto ours and get entangled in a win/lose contest. They win if we do what they think is best. And sometimes, we even resist really good advice because it means giving in to their wishes. Here again the ultimate test is in conversation with the Lord, facing Him with steady eyes.

The Lord has a plan for each of our lives. In addition to His will for our salvation and an intimate relationship with us, He has a personal will for each of us. Henry Drummond said, "There is a will of God for me which is willed for no one else besides. It is a particular will for me, different from the will He has for anyone else—a private will—a will which no one else knows about, which no one can know but me."

By private, Drummond did not mean the will that God reveals for us should never be talked about, but rather, that God has work for each of us to do. We can't receive guidance for others unless He confirms it in their own minds and hearts. The same is true for the guidance others may perceive for us.

A Warning: The Danger of Obstinacy

Now we are ready to consider being thankful for a warning. "Do not be like the horse or like the mule, which have no understanding, which must be harnessed with bit and bridle else they will not come near you." The focus is still on God guiding and teaching us the way to go. When we resist His guidance we are like a horse who will not respond to its master's beckoning eye. I think of my friend Roy Rogers, who could call Trigger to his side with a look and a nod of his head. Most horses are not that responsive. And all too often we are as unresponsive to God's guidance as a mule!

Obstinacy is the opposite of obedience. It is the will forcing its control over the mind and heart. We act like stubborn horses or mules that don't have understanding. I'm not saying that horses in particular, and mules in general, don't have intelligence. But they do lack understanding.

The word for *understanding* as it's used here in God's promise in Psalm 32 means more than comprehension. It means "agreement on a truth." When, on a human level, we say about another person, "We understand one another," we mean there are certain basic truths about life and each other that we hold in common. We may appreciate a horse's "sense" but we can't talk over with it where we are going or what route we will use to get there (unless we are going back to the barn!). The understanding the Lord says the horse and the mule do not have, and which He has given to us, is the ability to hear His word, see His eye, converse about what He wants us to be and do, and come to an understanding. The Greek word for "understanding" used in the Septuagint (the Greek translation of the Old Testament) for the Hebrew word in this verse is *suniemi*, "To bring or set together." It is used metaphorically of perceiving, and the agreement with what is perceived.

The Lord has created us to be able to think. The guidance of Scripture, the inspiration of the Holy Spirit, what we observe in the trend of circumstances, and the insight of wise friends, can all be used to bring us an understanding, an agreement with the Lord, about His will. Once that is established, our part is to obey.

The bit and bridle part of the equestrian simile is applicable to times when we refuse to live out the understanding we have gained in conversation with God. He must rein us in, or back, with His control. We've all known those times. The bit has a harsh bite; the bridle a chafing burn. But remember that the image of the bit and bridle is used by the Lord as the direct opposite of being guided by His eye.

Without carrying the imagery too far, it's helpful to remember that the Greek word used to record Jesus' Aramaic word for "meekness" is *praus*. And one of the definitions of *praus* is "leadability." A meek animal was responsive to its master's slightest touch on the reins without the use of the bit.

Christ taught that the meek inherit the earth, the fullness of God's blessings; He exemplified meekness with the Father as the Son of Man; and the Holy Spirit's fruit in us is meekness, one of Christ's own character traits.

It is with meekness that we respond to the Lord's offer to guide us. We submit to the reign of His reins. In reality, these reins are the gentle ties of His love.

> I've found a friend, O such a friend
> He loved me ere I knew Him.
> He drew me with the cords of love
> And thus He bound me to Him.
> And round my heart still closely twine
> Those ties which can't be severed.
> For I am His and He is mine
> Forever and forever!*

Daily Prayer for Guidance

The Lord draws us into conversation about His guidance so that He can help us anticipate decisions to be made and the direction to be taken. Daily conversations with Him take the panic out of getting guidance from the Lord.

Our usual pattern is to go along blithely, making our own plans and living our lives under our control. Then a crisis hits or

---

* James G. Small, "I've Found a Friend, O Such a Friend," first verse of hymn and poem.

an important decision must be made. Still we try to handle it ourselves. Then the deadline for some action or decision is pressed on us. Only now do we cry out for the Lord's help, and we want an immediate answer!

A much more creative way to live is to ask the Holy Spirit to guide us daily in anticipating choices and responses that will have to be made. He helps us by giving us lead time to express our need, to be open to conditioning thought and discernment, and then receive an inner assurance of what we are to say, do, or decide. Graciously, He guides us to Scriptures that will point the way, leads our silent meditation, and gives us a desire to do the will of God as He reveals it to us.

Eye to See God's Eye

Paul's prayer for the Ephesians is one of those biblical prayers we can pray with the first-person-singular intensity and intentionality we've discussed in each of the chapters of this book about conversation with God.

First look at the prayer as Paul prayed it for the Ephesians:

> That the God of our Lord Jesus Christ, the Father of glory, may give you the spirit of wisdom and revelation in the knowledge of Him, the eyes of your understanding being enlightened; that you may know what is the hope of His calling, what are the riches of the glory of His inheritance in the saints, and what is the exceeding greatness of His power toward us who believe, according to the working of His mighty power which He worked in Christ when He raised Him from the dead and seated Him at His right hand in heavenly places (Ephesians 1:17-20).

Before you pray that as your prayer, remember that there are eyes in your heart to see the eye of God who wants to guide you. Notice also the prayer that these eyes be "eyes of understanding." The Greek text reads, "The eyes of your hearts"—the heart being the seat of intellect, emotion, and will. Remember that understanding is agreement with God's revealed truth so you and the Lord can have an understanding. (It's more than "horse sense"!) He wants us to know where He is taking us and the power He provides to help get us there—nothing less than the same power that raised Jesus from the dead! Also, He wants to make us sure of our hope, and start drawing on the spiritual riches He's deposited in an account that can never be overdrawn—it has a direct spiritual computer link to the inheritance we now share with His Son. That should give us boldness to pray this prayer personally.

"God of my Lord Jesus Christ, the Father of glory, May You give me the Spirit of wisdom and revelation in the knowledge of Him, the eyes of my understanding being enlightened; that I may know what is the hope of my calling, what are the riches of the glory of His inheritance *(Christ's)* in the saints *(in me as one of them)* and what is the exceeding greatness of Your power in me who believes, according to the working of Your mighty power which You worked in Christ when You raised Him from the dead and seated Him at Your right hand in the heavenly places."

Now in the quiet of this moment, draw on your inheritance. Tell God how much you need His guidance. Ask for forgiveness for any time you expressed the obstinacy of not coming to Him or required the bit and bridle. Profess your willingness to be guided and instructed in the way you should go by His eye. Ask Him to prepare you for choices pressing in on you and decisions still ahead. Speak with Him eye-to-eye with the eyes of your heart.

And then for good measure, say out those great words of the psalmist, or sing them as spiritual songs:

> I delight to do Your will, O my God,
> And Your law is within my heart
> (Psalm 40:8).

Teach me to do Your will,
For You are my God;
Your Spirit is good.
Lead me in the land of uprightness
(Psalm 143:10).

10

The Conversation Calls for Commitment

I'll never forget it. It was four in the morning. The year, 1948. I paced back and forth in my dormitory room at Lake Forest College where I was a freshman.

Several hours before, two friends, Bruce Larson and Ralph Osborne, had given me a decisive challenge to make the most important decision of my life. In this challenge they had used a word that was foreign to both my understanding and experience. Commitment.

We had stayed up late talking about what it meant. Each of these men talked about their own experience of making a commitment. Finally they said, "Lloyd, eventually you must make a commitment of all that you know of yourself to all that you know of Christ."

I went back to my room with those strong, clear, simple words ringing in my ears. I couldn't sleep, so I paced, thinking over the implications of that commitment. Finally, at four in the morning, I got on my knees and committed my life to Christ. The adventure of discipleship began. Now all these years later, I can honestly say that the adventure only gets more exciting. Demanding, stretching, challenging—yes, all of that and more. But my commitment, ever deepening and constantly growing, is the same:

> I know whom I have believed and am persuaded that He is able to keep what I have committed to Him until that Day (2 Timothy 1:12).

Every day of my life I discover more of the Lord that calls for greater commitment, and I also realize more of myself that needs to be committed to Him. I've also learned that commitment is the open secret of living the abundant life. Hourly. Moment by moment. Commitment means surrendering myself to the Lord repeatedly, constantly, in the relationships and responsibilities of my life.

Commitment is also the final step in our daily time alone with God in the conversation of prayer. Everything we learn from the Lord in each aspect of that conversation must be lived. That requires commitment. Effective growth in the school of prayer requires application of the discoveries we make in prayer. With the Lord we are always interns, constantly learning and living what we've been taught under the supervision of our Master, Teacher, and Lord. He will never lead us beyond where His grace will sustain us.

Our Concluding Commitment

We conclude a conversation with God by saying, "In Christ's Name," or "Through the Name of Jesus Christ, our Lord." The name means authority and power. We need the authority of the name of Christ, our Advocate with the Father, for our prayers to be effective; we need His power to live the prayers we've prayed. He says,

> Whatever you ask in My name, that I will do, that the Father may be glorified in the Son. If you ask anything in My name, I will do it (John 14:13-14).

Then, in the same breath, He continues with what requires our commitment.

> If you love Me, keep My commandments (verse 15).

We don't have to look far to find the central thrust of His commandments:

> This is My commandment, that you love one another as I have loved you (John 15:12).

Love is the essence of commitment. Loving others as Christ has loved us spells out the cost of discipleship, our desire to share what He means to us, our servanthood in the problems of society, our radical obedience to Him in all of life.

Our Continuing Commitment

We don't ever really end the conversation of prayer. It might be better to say, "To be continued in Christ's name." All of life is to be saturated with constant prayer. The ordered conversation of prayer we've discussed prepares the rest of the hours of the day to be fresh opportunities to live out with people the commitment we have made alone with the Lord.

Our Lord cannot be excluded from any place, situation, circumstance, problem or relationship. He is in every place before we get there; with every person before we try to relate or communicate; available in every complexity or pain we face. And to appropriate the power He offers requires complete and constant commitment.

Understanding Commitment

But let's be sure we understand what commitment means. The word has the ring of something we accomplish by ourselves for the Lord. He gives the orders; we take the command; we do our best to work it out with our strength; we check back in for new instructions when we've finished the assignments He's laid out for us. That's a dangerous misunderstanding of commitment.

Commitment is the liberation step of prayer. It is relinquishing to the Lord's control ourselves, others, our needs, and especially our fears and frustrations. The Hebrew word for *commit* is literally "roll," as though we roll over onto the Lord a burden. Picture rolling your burdens over onto the back of our Lord. Surrender them to Him. Commitment is the missing, releasing step in so many prayers. Anything worth praying about requires commitment. It leads to openness.

What are the problems and perplexities on your mind right now? In what areas are you clenching your fists and saying, "I've got to take care of this on my own"? Open those fists and put the needs into the trustworthy hands of our Lord. He is worthy of the trust. He's been handling people and problems since the beginning of time. He is able!

As I put a comma at the end of a conversation with the Lord, I often repeat the "He is able" affirmation of the writers of the epistles. They remind me that my commitment is to a Lord who has all power. The word *able* in Greek is *dunameno*, from *dunamis*, power. The following verses are heartening to repeat as we say, "To be continued..." at the conclusion of a time alone with our Lord:

> [He] is able to do exceedingly abundantly above all that we ask or think, according to the power that works in us (Ephesians 3:20).
>
> He is able even to subdue all things to Himself (Philippians 3:21).
>
> He is able to aid those who are tempted (Hebrews 2:18).
>
> He is also able to save to the uttermost (Hebrews 7:25).
>
> [He] is able to keep you from stumbling (Jude 24).
>
> [He] is able to establish you (Romans 16:25).
>
> He is able to keep what I have committed to Him (2 Timothy 1:12).*

The last on the list of "He is able" affirmations is the one I quoted earlier in this chapter as my life verse, and it can also be translated: "He is able to keep what He has committed to me." That leads us on to the dual meaning of commitment.

---

* For a comprehensive exposition of the "He is able" ascriptions, see my book *Lord of the Loose Ends* (Waco, TX: Word, Inc., 1991).

What Our Lord Commits to Us

When we commit our lives and all our needs and concerns on a daily basis, He does entrust them back to us to do what He wills with His constant guidance and power. He *is* able to keep what He commits to us. The Greek word for *keep* is *phulasso,* denoting to guard, watch, protect. In the ancient banking world it meant to care for a person's investment and be sure it multiplied with interest. Our Lord guards what we commit to Him and what He subsequently commits to us to do. He multiplies the strength and courage to follow His direction.

Let's see how this works. During the steps of conversation in prayer, after preparation, praise, confession, and thanksgiving, we were silent—seeking to listen to the Lord before the subsequent steps of intercession and supplication. Then with a serious quest to know the will of God, we prayed for guidance. Specific things that are committed for us to do and be became clear. Now we commit ourselves to obedient follow-through. At the same time the Lord honors our commitment by committing to us His faithfulness and the guidance and energizing power of the Holy Spirit. We are never left on our own to struggle or blunder through. We have the Father watching over us, Christ before us leading the way, and the Holy Spirit within us, giving us the will and courage to follow.

Now consider how this dual commitment to God and His commitment to undertake to help us is worked out in our basic relationships with ourselves, others, the church, and the world.

A vital part of our ministry to people is sharing what God means to us. The challenge of the angel to Peter and John when they were released from prison is a great watchword for us when we are released from the prison of "self"—and self-centeredness: "Go tell all the people about this new life" (Acts 5:20 TEV). We can do that when we have Paul's conviction and commitment. "For to me, to live is Christ" (Philippians 1:21).

In our conversation with God, we've had to confront attitudes, values, actions, and personality proclivities that He has shown us need to be changed. When we really want to be different, we confess and give up any distortions and commit them to Him. He releases the power to change.

Or when we pray about the people in our lives, God not only helps us picture and claim His best for them, He puts us into the picture showing us what He wants us to do to assist and encourage them. He reveals what love demands of us in a relationship with a specific person about whom we have prayed. What we are commissioned to do or say may be completely contrary to our inclination based on our judgments or impatience. When it becomes clear what we are to do and say, we commit the challenge back to the Lord. He gives us strength to act.

Now think of the church. Our prayers often focus on problems; the Lord directs our attention to the potential. Instead of hopping from one church to another, He guides us to what we are to do as a part of His strategy or renewal in our congregation. We are challenged to ask, "If the entire congregation had my level of faith, vision, and involvement, what kind of church would we have?"

Think of that in terms of your willingness for your congregation to be on fire for the gospel, open to revival, free in the Spirit, generous with tithes and offerings, on the move in personal evangelism and mission, flexible to enjoy new ways of worship, and spontaneous in really caring about fellow members. The answer can be alarming, but it can also lead to commitment to be the kind of member the Lord wants us to be. And because the Lord loves the church, He will commit to us exactly what we need.

In regard to our communities, our tendency is to wring our hands in consternation. For example, the Los Angeles riots in May 1992 were a wake-up call to Christians here. We had to confront the problems of racism, poverty, injustice, unemployment, hunger, and homelessness in our city. We were also confronted with a raw exposure to the lawlessness of looters and rioters. In my church we prayed for guidance about what each of us could do, and together we prayed for our congregation's role in the crisis. The Lord made the direction very clear. The first step was to repent for any neglect or latent racism in us. Then we had to act. While the city still smoldered, van after van full of food and clothing were sent. Money was collected and given. An interracial and intercultural meeting of more than seven hundred pastors gathered in our sanctuary to pray and seek long-range solutions to the problems that had erupted. The Lord called for our commitment to what He guided us to do; our commitment opened the floodgate of resources.

The plumb line of the Lord's justice and righteousness must be lowered on the cities of our nation. And as we see what's out of plumb, we are summoned to pray for what the Lord puts on our agenda to do. The knowledge of a need is a call to commitment if the Lord puts that need on our hearts. To refuse is perilous for our relationship with Him; to respond is to become a channel for the flow of immense power.

The power Christ promised is for servanthood, not for our personal aggrandizement. At every point in His message is a call to action. At the end of the Sermon on the Mount, He mandated both hearing and doing:

> Therefore whoever hears these sayings of Mine, and does them, I will liken him to a wise man who built his house on a rock: and the rain descended, the floods came, and the winds blew and beat on that house; and it did not fall, for it was founded on the rock. But everyone who hears these sayings of Mine, and does not do them, will be like a foolish man who built his house on the sand: and the rain descended, the floods came, and the winds blew and beat on that house, and it fell. And great was its fall (Matthew 7:24-27).

The thrust of so many of Jesus' parables call for a commitment to act; to invest and multiply the talent entrusted to us, to claim the kingdom within and expand its reaches to every area of personal and social life.

One of the parables is particularly pointed. A man with two sons called them both to work in his vineyard. One said, "I will not," but later regretted his resistance and went to work. The other responded with a facile, slippery, solicitous "I will go, sir," but never went to work in the vineyard.

Jesus' question was penetrating: "Which of the two sons did the will of his father?"

The crowd of Jesus' listeners that included the religious scribes and Pharisees, responded, "The first." The Master's retort was, "Most assuredly I say to you that tax collectors and harlots enter the Kingdom of God before you."

The central point was that neither son really did the will of the father in the parable. His will was that both sons work with him in the vineyard with alacrity. After all, the vineyard was a family business that the sons would inherit. It was in their own interest to make it the finest vineyard in the land.

In the same way we inherit the Kingdom of God. The life we are given is a trust. Seeking the Lord's will and doing it, working in "The vineyard" of our family, relationships, work, and community, should be our joy.

And yet when we are called, so often our response is, "Of course, Lord, I will," but then we find excuses for not doing what we promised. And those of us who are always dragging our feet are no better, even if we finally do what we are commanded.

There was a third son *not* mentioned in the parable. Jesus hoped they'd see the deeper implication. It was He! He had given the example all through His life of obedience to the heavenly Father. He didn't need to be convinced to work in the vineyard. And He called people to follow Him who were ready to put the kingdom first in their lives.

When the Master finished washing the disciples' feet, He said something that should be the call to commitment at the "To be continued" close for the conversation of prayer.

> Do you know what I have done to you? You call Me Teacher and Lord, and you say well, for so I am. If I then, your Lord and Teacher, have washed your feet, you also ought to wash one

another's feet. I have given you an example, that you should do as I have done to you. Most assuredly, I say to you, a servant is not greater than his master; nor is he who is sent greater than he who sent him. If you know these things, *[happy] are you if you do them* (John 13:12-17).

The Blessed Do!

The same word translated "happy" is the word for *blessed* in the Beatitudes. The truly blessed *do* the things they know. They are the people with an indefatigable joy, an unsurpassable happiness. It's rooted in the wondrous security of knowing that we are elected, called, cherished—the blessed, indeed. And that blessedness makes commitment a ready response. It is fully realized, moment by moment, as we do what the Lord commands in our prayers. It will always be some kind of foot-washing role of a servant. Washing the feet of others means really listening and caring, and then giving ourselves away to help them. And happy are we when we do what love demands!

The awesome thing is the way Christ personalizes commitment to serve. What we do for others, we do for Him. He comes to us in our mates, children, friends, people at work; and He has a surprising way of appearing in both the down-and-outer and the up-and-outer. And His question to Peter is His question to us, "Do you love Me?" If we do, people and their needs will be our agenda.

Remember the formula: Commit what the Lord commits to us, and He will commit His unlimited grace to help us put our prayers into action.

With that assurance we can employ some instigating "self-talk" to ourselves using two of the impelling calls to commitment in Scripture:

Commit your way to the LORD, trust also in Him, and He shall bring it to pass....Rest in the LORD, and wait patiently for Him (Psalm 37:5,7).

> Commit your works to the LORD, and your thoughts will be established (Proverbs 16:3).

No prayer is complete without waiting for the Lord's promised power. Empowerment comes with the anointing of the Spirit. The Lord says, "As your days, so shall your strength be" (Deuteronomy 33:25). He will give us exactly what we need each day.

Jesus promised,

> "He who believes in Me, as the Scripture has said, out of his heart will flow rivers of living water." But this He spoke concerning the Spirit, whom those believing in Him would receive (John 7:38-39).

The river of the Spirit gushes into and fills the inner needs we have talked to the Lord about in our conversation with Him. Like an artesian geyser, the Spirit fills our empty wells of uncertainty, worry, and fear. Guidance is given and our intellectual abilities are maximized. Our memories are healed and our emotions are liberated; our physical bodies receive new resiliency and health.

Our conversation with God has made us ready to live again. It has brought new visions of what we can be, fresh challenges of what we are to do, great expectations of what the future holds. And we can press on knowing that the Lord provides for what He guides.

Now I pray that you can understand why I opened this book by saying that nothing is more important than a daily conversation alone with God. And it always ends with, "To be continued...in Jesus' name and with the power of the Holy Spirit!"

Part Two

Using
Scripture
to Listen
and
Respond

Thirty Days
that Could
Change
Your Life

So many books on prayer give us helpful theories about prayer, but leave us adrift when it comes to actually praying. We have discussed prayer as conversation with God, utilizing the Scriptures to listen and respond in each stage of this privilege of talking with God. We have affirmed that the Bible is the inspired Word of God in which He speaks to us and from which we find words to reply. These responses give wings to our own words.

This method of conversing with God may be new to some. I hope the chapters of this book and the explanation of each phase of a biblically rooted conversation with God has created a desire to try it yourself. However, finding the powerful promises and resilient responses may prove difficult at first. While a concordance is helpful, it's not always handy.

For this reason I have assembled Scriptures for each of the steps of conversation with God to help you for the next thirty days. I began this method of using Scriptures as the launching pad for listening and responding to God years ago. Through these many years of the adventure, I've found verses and passages I had not appropriated before. I've put these under the headings of the steps of prayer outlined in this book. There is a word from the Lord and a response in each. Pause to meditate on the meaning of each verse or passage. Let the conversation flow between you and God. Sometimes you will want to refer back to the chapter explaining a particular phase of the conversation to heighten your awareness of what it can mean to you.

Putting some of the response Scriptures in the first person singular is something I've done for the past twenty years. I've found it invaluable in claiming personally the truth or assurance which appears in second or third person in the verse or passage. I've illustrated how to do this in the chapters of this book. I'd encourage you to try it.

You may want to repeat the month's plan over and over until these Scriptures become a memorized part of your spiritual resources for living life as a "To be continued," never completed flow of exchange with God all through your days.

My fondest hope is that this book will be a kind of contemporary prayer book for you, a companion to your Bible, and a guide for daily conversations with God.

Day One

Preparation

Listen: "It shall come to pass that before they call I will answer; and while they are still speaking, I will hear" (Isaiah 65:24).

"Then you will call upon Me and go and pray to Me, and I will listen to you" (Jeremiah 29:12).

Response: "As the deer pants for the water brooks, so pants my soul for You, O God. My soul thirsts for God, for the living God" (Psalm 42:1-2).

"Bless the Lord, O my soul; and all that is within me, bless His holy name. Bless the Lord, O my soul, and forget not all His benefits: who forgives all your iniquities, who heals all your diseases, who redeems your life from destruction, who crowns you with lovingkindness and tender mercies" (Psalm 103:1-2).

Praise

Listen: "'But let him who glories glory in this, that he understands and knows Me, that I am the Lord, exercising lovingkindness, judgment, and righteousness in the earth. For in these I delight,' says the Lord" (Jeremiah 9:24).

Response: "I will praise You, O LORD, with my whole heart; I will tell of all Your marvelous works. I will be glad and rejoice in You; I will sing praise to Your Name, O Most High" (Psalm 9:1-2).

"Because Your lovingkindness is better than life, my lips shall praise You. Thus I will bless You while I live" (Psalm 63:3-4a).

Now praise the Lord for Himself in your own words of adoration.

Confession

Listen: "If My people who are called by My Name will humble themselves, and pray and seek My face, and turn from their wicked ways, then I will hear from heaven, and will forgive their sin and heal their land" (2 Chronicles 7:14).

"Therefore speak to them, and say to them, 'Thus says the Lord GOD: "Everyone of the house of Israel who sets up his idols in his heart, and puts before him what causes him to stumble into iniquity, and then comes to the prophet, I the LORD will answer him who comes, according to the multitude of his idols, that I may seize the house of Israel by their heart, because they are all estranged from Me by their idols"'"(Ezekiel 14:4-5).

Response: If I say that I have no sin, I deceive myself, and the truth is not in me. If I confess my sins, He is faithful and just to forgive me of my sins and to cleanse me from all unrighteousness (see 1 John 1:8-9).

"For as the heavens are high above the earth, so great is His mercy toward those who fear Him; as far as the east is from the west, so far has He removed our transgressions from us" (Psalm 103:11-12).

Now confess whatever the Lord has shown you that needs His forgiveness.

Thanksgiving

Listen: "Enter into His gates with thanksgiving, and into His courts with praise. Be thankful to Him, and bless His name. For the LORD is good; His mercy is everlasting, and His truth endures to all generations" (Psalm 100:4-5).

"So you shall rejoice in every good thing which the LORD your God has given you" (Deuteronomy 26:11).

Response: "To Him who loved us and washed us from our sins in His own blood, and has made us kings and priests to His God and Father, to Him be glory and dominion forever and ever. Amen" (Revelation 1:5-6).

Now list out in your mind the blessings of God for which you are thankful today and thank Him with a grateful heart.

Silence

Listen: "Keep silence before Me, O coastlands, and let the people renew their strength! Let them come near, then let them speak; let us come near together for judgment" (Isaiah 41:1).

"If any of you lacks wisdom, let him ask of God, who gives to all liberally and without reproach, and it will be given to him" (James 1:5).

Response: I will trust in the Lord with all of my heart, and lean not on my own understanding; in all my ways, I will acknowledge Him, and He shall direct my path (see Proverbs 3:5-6).

Now be silent and listen as you meditate. Ask the Lord to guide your reflection about the needs of others, and what He has to say about what He wants you to be and do.

Intercession

Listen: "Most assuredly, I say to you, he who believes in Me, the works that I do he will do also; and greater works than these he will do, because I go to My Father. And whatever you ask in My name, that I will do, that the Father may be glorified in the Son. If you ask anything in My name, I will do it. If you love Me, keep My commandments" (John 14:12-15).

"Likewise the Spirit also helps in our weaknesses. For we do not know what we should pray for as we ought, but the Spirit Himself makes intercession for us with groanings which cannot be uttered. Now He who searches the heart knows what the mind of the Spirit is, because He makes intercession for the saints according to the will of God" (Romans 8:26-27).

Response: I do not cease to pray for you (see Colossians 1:9).

"I thank my God upon every remembrance of you, always in every prayer of mine making request for you all with joy" (Philippians 1:3-4).

Now intercede for family, friends, people in special need, and the sick.

Supplication

Listen: "Peace I leave with you, My peace I give to you; not as the world gives do I give to you. Let not your heart be troubled, neither let it be afraid" (John 14:27).

"Cast your burden on the LORD, and He shall sustain you" (Psalm 55:22).

Response: I will be anxious for nothing, but in everything by prayer and supplication, with thanksgiving, I will let my requests be made known to God; and the peace of God, which surpasses all understanding, will guard my heart and mind through Christ Jesus (see Philippians 4:6-7).

Now pray for your deepest needs, thanking the Lord for His care.

Guidance

Listen: "I will instruct you and teach you in the way you should go; I will guide you with My eye. Do not be like the horse or like the mule, which have no understanding, which must be harnessed with bit and bridle, else they will not come near you" (Psalm 32:8-9).

Response: God of my Lord Jesus Christ, the Father of glory, may You give me the Spirit of wisdom and revelation in the knowledge of Him, the eyes of my understanding being enlightened; that I may know what is the hope of my calling, what are the riches of the glory of Your inheritance in the saints, and what is the exceeding greatness of Your power in me who believes, according to the working of Your mighty power which You worked in Christ when You raised Him from the dead and seated Him at Your right hand in the heavenly places (see Ephesians 1:17-20).

Now pray for specific responsibilities and relationships in which you need guidance.

Commitment and Empowering

Listen: "You call Me Teacher and Lord, and you say well, for so I am. If I, then, your Lord and Teacher, have washed your feet, you also ought to wash one another's feet. For I have given you an example, that you should do as I have done to you. Most assuredly, I say to you, a servant is not greater than his master; nor is he who is sent greater than He who sent him. If you know these things, blessed are you if you do them" (John 13:13-17).

"Commit your way to the LORD, trust also in Him, and He shall bring it to pass....Rest in the LORD, and wait patiently for Him" (Psalm 37:5,7).

"Commit your works to the LORD, and your thoughts will be established" (Proverbs 16:3).

Response: "For I know whom I have believed and am persuaded that He is able to keep what I have committed to Him until that Day" (2 Timothy 1:12).

"I can do all things through Christ who strengthens me" (Philippians 4:13).

"As your days, so shall your strength be" (Deuteronomy 33:25).

Now commit your life anew, surrender the needs of the day ahead, and trust the Lord completely.

Day Two

Preparation

Listen: "Fear not, for I am with you; be not dismayed, for I am your God. I will strengthen you, yes, I will help you, I will uphold you with My righteous right hand" (Isaiah 41:10).

Response: "I will lift up my eyes to the hills—from whence comes my help?" (Psalm 121:1).

Praise

Listen: "Be still, and know that I am God; I will be exalted among the nations, I will be exalted in the earth!" (Psalm 46:10).

Response: "I will praise You with my whole heart; before the gods I will sing praises to You. I will worship toward Your holy temple, and praise Your name for Your loving-kindness and Your truth; for You have magnified Your word above all Your name. In the day when I cried out, You answered me, and made me bold with strength in my soul" (Psalm 138:1-3).

Now praise the Lord with freedom and joy.

Confession

Listen: " 'Come now, and let us reason together,' says the
LORD. 'Though your sins are like scarlet, they shall be
white as snow; though they are red like crimson, they
shall be as wool' " (Isaiah 1:18).

Response: "Out of the depths I have cried to You, O LORD; Lord,
hear my voice! Let Your ears be attentive to the voice of
my supplications. If You, LORD, should mark iniquities, O Lord, who could stand? But there is forgiveness
with You, that You may be feared" (Psalm 130:1-4).

*Now allow the Lord to guide you in your confession. Ask
Him to reveal to you anything that stands between you
and Him. Then forgive others as He has forgiven you.*

Thanksgiving

Listen: "I have loved you with an everlasting love; therefore with
lovingkindness I have drawn you" (Jeremiah 31:3).

Response: "How precious is Your lovingkindness, O God" (Psalm
36:7).

"Because Your lovingkindness is better than life, my
lips shall praise You. Thus I will bless You while I live; I
will lift up my hands in Your name" (Psalm 63:3-4).

"It is good to give thanks to the LORD, and to sing
praises to Your name, O Most High; to declare Your
lovingkindness in the morning, and Your faithfulness
every night" (Psalm 92:1-2).

*Now, in the presence of the Lord, think of His loving-
kindness to you and give thanks.*

Silence

Listen: "The LORD is in His holy temple. Let all the earth keep
silence before Him" (Habakkuk 2:20).

"The LORD your God in your midst, the Mighty One will save; He will rejoice over you with gladness, He will quiet you with His love, He will rejoice over you with singing" (Zephaniah 3:17).

Response: "Show me Your ways, O LORD; teach me Your paths. Lead me in Your truth and teach me, for You are the God of my salvation; on You I wait all the day" (Psalm 25:4-5).

In the silence, allow the Lord to picture what you are to ask for others and yourself.

Intercession

Listen: "Bear one another's burdens, and so fulfill the law of Christ" (Galatians 6:2).

Response: "As for me, far be it from me that I should sin against the LORD in ceasing to pray for you" (1 Samuel 12:23).

Now pray for your family, friends, enemies, those you need to learn to love, your church, your pastor, and church leaders, and the president, governor, and leaders of your city.

Supplication

Listen: "Ask, and it will be given to you; seek, and you will find; knock, and it will be opened to you. For everyone who asks receives, and he who seeks finds, and to him who knocks it will be opened. Or what man is there among you who, if his son asks for bread, will give him a stone? Or if he asks for a fish, will he give him a serpent? If you then, being evil, know how to give good gifts to your children, how much more will your Father who is in heaven give good things to those who ask Him!" (Matthew 7:7-11).

> "You therefore, my son, be strong in the grace that is in Christ Jesus" (2 Timothy 2:1).

Response: "Give ear, O LORD, to my prayer; and attend to the voice of my supplications. In the day of my trouble I will call upon You, for You will answer me" (Psalm 86:6-7).

Now list out your needs and thank the Lord in advance for His answers in His timing.

Guidance

Listen: "If you abide in My word, you are My disciples indeed. And you shall know the truth, and the truth shall make you free" (John 8:31-32).

"Your kingdom come. Your will be done on earth as it is in heaven" (Matthew 6:10).

Response: "I delight to do Your will, O my God, and Your law is within my heart" (Psalm 40:8).

Now spread out all the decisions you must make and ask the Lord to guide you.

Commitment and Empowerment

Listen: "Then Jesus said to His disciples, 'If anyone desires to come after Me, let him deny himself, and take up his cross, and follow Me. For whoever desires to save his life will lose it, and whoever loses his life for My sake will find it. For what profit is it to a man if he gains the whole world, and loses his own soul? Or what will a man give in exchange for his soul?'" (Matthew 16:24-26).

Response: "I have been crucified with Christ; it is no longer I who live, but Christ lives in me; and the life which I now live in the flesh I live by faith in the Son of God, who loved me and gave Himself for me" (Galatians 2:20).

Now commit to the Lord your day and all you are to do and be to His glory.

Day
Three

Preparation

Listen: "But now, thus says the LORD, who created you... 'Fear not, for I have redeemed you; I have called you by your name; you are Mine'" (Isaiah 43:1).

Response: "O LORD, our Lord, how excellent is Your name in all the earth, Who have set Your glory above the heavens! Out of the mouth of babes and infants You have ordained strength, because of Your enemies, that you may silence the enemy and the avenger. When I consider Your heavens, the work of Your fingers, the moon and the stars, which You have ordained, what is man that You are mindful of him, and the son of man that You visit him? For You have made him a little lower than the angels, and You have crowned him with glory and honor. You have made him to have dominion over the works of Your hands; You have put all things under his feet, all sheep and oxen—even the beasts of the field, the birds of the air, and the fish of the sea that pass through the paths of the seas. O LORD, our Lord, how excellent is Your name in all the earth!" (Psalm 8).

Praise

Listen: "Yet I will not forget you. See, I have inscribed you in the palms of My hands; your walls are continually before Me" (Isaiah 49:15-16).

Response: "I will bless the LORD at all times; His praise shall continually be in my mouth. My soul shall make its boast in the LORD; the humble shall hear of it and be glad. Oh, magnify the LORD with me, and let us exalt His name together" (Psalm 34:1-3).

"Let everything that has breath praise the LORD. Praise the LORD!" (Psalm 150:6).

Now tell the Lord how much you love Him.

Confession

Listen: "The LORD is gracious and full of compassion, slow to anger and great in mercy. The LORD is good to all, and His tender mercies are over all His works" (Psalm 145:8-9).

Response: "But now the righteousness of God apart from the law is revealed, being witnessed by the Law and the Prophets, even the righteousness of God which is through faith in Jesus Christ, to all and on all who believe. For there is no difference; for all have sinned and fall short of the glory of God, being justified freely by His grace through the redemption that is in Christ Jesus, whom God set forth as a propitiation by His blood, through faith, to demonstrate His righteousness, because in His forbearance God had passed over the sins that were previously committed, to demonstrate at the present time His righteousness, that He might be just and the justifier of the one who has faith in Jesus" (Romans 3:21-26).

Remember: Confession is to say after the Lord what He has shown you needs His forgiveness. Ask Him to put on your mind what needs to be confessed to Him and then claim His assurance of pardon.

Thanksgiving

Listen: "What then shall we say to these things? If God is for us, who can be against us? He who did not spare His own Son, but delivered Him up for us all, how shall He not with Him also freely give us all things? Who shall bring a charge against God's elect? It is God who justifies. Who is he who condemns? It is Christ who died, and furthermore is also risen, who is even at the right hand of God, who also makes intercession for us. Who shall separate us from the love of Christ? Shall tribulation, or distress, or persecution, or famine, or nakedness, or peril, or sword?" (Romans 8:31-35).

Response: "Yet in all these things we are more than conquerors through Him who loved us. For I am persuaded that neither death nor life, nor angels nor principalities nor powers, nor things present nor things to come, nor height nor depth, nor any other created thing, shall be able to separate us from the love of God which is in Christ Jesus our Lord" (Romans 8:37-39).

Write out a list of the Lord's blessings and allow your heart to soar in gratitude as you thank Him.

Silence

Listen: "Listen now to my voice" (Exodus 18:19).

Response: "Let the words of my mouth and the meditation of my heart be acceptable in Your sight, O LORD, my strength and my Redeemer" (Psalm 19:14).

Allow the Lord to use your imagination to picture what

He wants you to do and say in the challenges and opportunities of this day.

Intercession

Listen: "Now this is the confidence that we may have in Him, that if we ask anything according to His will, He hears us. And if we know that He hears us, whatever we ask, we know that we have the petitions that we have asked of Him" (1 John 5:14-15).

Response: "For God is my witness, whom I serve with my spirit in the gospel of His Son, that without ceasing I make mention of you always in my prayers" (Romans 1:9).

Now claim the Lord's maximum blessings for those on your mind today.

Supplication

Listen: "The LORD is near to all who call upon Him, to all who call upon Him in truth. He will fulfill the desire of those who fear Him; He also will hear their cry and save them" (Psalm 145:18-19).

Response: "Out of the depths I have cried to You, O LORD; Lord, hear my voice! Let your ears be attentive to the voice of my supplications" (Psalm 130:1-2).

Place in the Lord's hands all your concerns and trust Him.

Guidance

Listen: "Then Jesus spoke to them again, saying, 'I am the light of the world. He who follows Me shall not walk in darkness, but have the light of life'" (John 8:12).

Response: "The LORD is my light and my salvation; whom shall I fear? The Lord is the strength of my life; of whom shall I be afraid?" (Psalm 27:1).

Now, listen to the Lord for specific steps you are to take.

Commitment and Empowering

Listen: "So Jesus said to them, '...if you have faith as a mustard seed, you will say to this mountain, "Move from here to there," and it will move; and nothing will be impossible for you'" (Matthew 17:20).

Response: "[He] is able to do exceedingly abundantly above all that we ask or think, according to the power that works in us" (Ephesians 3:20).

"He is able even to subdue all things to Himself " (Philippians 3:21).

"He is able to aid those who are tempted" (Hebrews 2:18).

"He is...able to save to the uttermost" (Hebrews 7:25).

"[He] is able to keep you from stumbling" (Jude 24).

"[He] is able to establish you" (Romans 16:25).

"He is able to keep what I have committed to Him" (2 Timothy 1:12).

Now commit your day to the Lord. He is able!

Day Four

Preparation

Listen: "I will give you a new heart and put a new spirit within you; I will take the heart of stone out of your flesh and give you a heart of flesh. I will put My Spirit within you and cause you to walk in My statutes, and you will keep My judgments and do them" (Ezekiel 36:26-27).

Response: "Through the LORD's mercies we are not consumed, because His compassions fail not. They are new every morning; great is Your faithfulness. 'The LORD is my portion,' says my soul, 'therefore I hope in Him!'" (Lamentations 3:22-25).

Praise

Listen: "Praise the LORD! I will praise the LORD with my whole heart" (Psalm 111:1).

Response: "I will praise You, O Lord my God, with all my heart, and I will glorify Your name forevermore" (Psalm 86:12).

Think magnificently of God—His attributes, His nature, and His glory, and then praise Him with your whole heart.

Confession

Listen: "'Now, therefore,' says the LORD, 'Turn to Me with all

your heart....' So rend your heart, and not your garments; return to the LORD your God, for He is gracious
and merciful, slow to anger, and of great kindness; and
He relents from doing harm" (Joel 2:12-13).

Response: "Purge me with hyssop, and I shall be clean; wash me,
and I shall be whiter than snow. Make me hear joy
and gladness, that the bones You have broken may
rejoice. Hide Your face from my sins, and blot out all
my iniquities. Create in me a clean heart, O God, and
renew a steadfast spirit within me" (Psalm 51:7-10).

*Claim the forgiveness of what you have done or said that
needs His forgiveness.*

Thanksgiving

Listen: "Oh, give thanks to the LORD, for He is good! For His
mercy endures forever" (1 Chronicles 16:34).

Response: "Oh, give thanks to the LORD! Call upon His name;
make known His deeds among the peoples! Sing to
Him, sing psalms to Him; talk of all His wondrous
works! Glory in His holy name; let the hearts of those
rejoice who seek the LORD! Seek the LORD and His
strength; seek His face evermore! Remember His
marvelous works which He has done" (1 Chronicles
16:8-12).

*Thanksgiving is the memory of the heart. Remember what
the Lord has done for you and express your gratitude.*

Silence

Listen: "Meditate within your heart on your bed, and be still.
Offer the sacrifices of righteousness, and put your trust
in the LORD" (Psalm 4:4-5).

Response: "I meditate within my heart, and my spirit makes diligent search" (Psalm 77:6).

Picture your life completely under the control of the Lord. Seeking first His kingdom, what needs to be changed, renewed, released?

Intercession

Listen: "'And you shall love the LORD your God with all your heart, with all your soul, with all your mind, and with all your strength.' This is the first commandment. And the second, like it, is this: 'You shall love your neighbor as yourself.' There is no other commandment greater than these" (Mark 12:30-31).

Response: "Being confident of this very thing, that He who has begun a good work in you will complete it until the day of Jesus Christ; just as it is right for me to think this of you all, because I have you in my heart" (Philippians 1:6-7).

Now pray specifically for family members, friends, people at work, those in government, the church, and those who have special physical or spiritual needs.

Supplication

Listen: "Delight yourself also in the LORD, and He shall give you the desires of your heart" (Psalm 37:4).

Response: "Therefore, having been justified by faith, we have peace with God through our Lord Jesus Christ, through whom also we have access by faith into this grace in which we stand, and rejoice in hope of the glory of God. And not only that, but we also glory in tribulations, knowing that tribulation produces perseverance; and perseverance, character; and character, hope. Now hope does not disappoint, because the love of God has been poured out in our hearts by the Holy Spirit who was given to us" (Romans 5:1-5).

Open your heart to the Lord and trust Him with whatever causes you worry or anxiety today.

Guidance

Listen:　"Peace I leave with you, My peace I give to you; not as the world gives do I give to you. Let not your heart be troubled, neither let it be afraid" (John 14:27).

Response:　"I delight to do Your will, O my God, and Your law is within my heart" (Psalm 40:8).

Now ask the Lord for the steps He wants you to take today.

Commitment and Empowering

Listen:　"'He who believes in Me, as the Scripture has said, out of his heart will flow rivers of living water.' But this He spoke concerning the Spirit, whom those believing in Him would receive; for the Holy Spirit was not yet given, because Jesus was not yet glorified" (John 7:38-39).

Response:　For this reason I bow my knees to the Father of our Lord Jesus Christ, from whom the whole family of heaven and earth is named, that He would grant me, according to the riches of His glory, to be strengthened with might through His Spirit in the inner man, that Christ may dwell in my heart through faith, that I, being rooted and grounded in love, may be able to comprehend with all the saints what is the width and length and depth and height—to know the love of

Christ which passes knowledge; that I may be filled with all the fullness of God. Now to Him who is able to do exceedingly abundantly above all that I ask or think, according to the power that works in me, to Him be glory in the church by Christ Jesus to all generations, forever and ever. Amen (see Ephesians 3:14-20).

The Lord gives the day; He will show the way.

Day Five

Preparation

Listen: "I will lift up my eyes to the hills—from whence comes my help? My help comes from the LORD, who made heaven and earth. He will not allow your foot to be moved; He who keeps you will not slumber. Behold, He who keeps Israel shall neither slumber nor sleep. The LORD is your keeper: the LORD is your shade at your right hand. The sun shall not strike you by day, nor the moon by night. The LORD shall preserve you from all evil; He shall preserve your soul. The LORD shall preserve your going out and your coming in from this time forth, and even forevermore" (Psalm 121).

Response: "Why are you cast down, O my soul? And why are you disquieted within me? Hope in God; for I shall yet praise Him, the help of my countenance and my God" (Psalm 42:11).

Praise

Listen: "Because the foolishness of God is wiser than men, and the weakness of God is stronger than men. For you see your calling, brethren, that not many wise according to the flesh, not many mighty, not many noble, are called. But God has chosen the foolish things of the

world to put to shame the wise, and God has chosen the weak things of the world to put to shame the things which are mighty; and the base things of the world and the things which are despised God has chosen, and the things which are not, to bring to nothing the things that are, that no flesh should glory in His presence. But of Him you are in Christ Jesus, who became for us wisdom from God—and a righteousness and sanctification and redemption—that, as it is written, 'He who glories, let him glory in the Lord'"
(1 Corinthians 1:25-31).

Response: "I thank You and praise You, O God of my fathers; You have given me wisdom and might" (Daniel 2:23).

Now take time to glorify and enjoy the Lord.

Confession

Listen: "Woe to those who call evil good, and good evil; who put darkness for light, and light for darkness; who put bitter for sweet, and sweet for bitter! Woe to those who are wise in their own eyes, and prudent in their own sight" (Isaiah 5:20-21).

Response: I will not be wise in my own opinion (see Romans 12:16).

Now allow the Lord to reveal any disobedience or unwillingness to do His will.

Thanksgiving

Listen: "I will call upon the LORD, who is worthy to be praised; so shall I be saved from my enemies"
(2 Samuel 22:4).

Response: "For who is God, except the LORD? And who is a rock, except our God? God is my strength and power, and

He makes my way perfect. He makes my feet like the feet of deer, and sets me on my high places" (2 Samuel 22:32-34).

Now thank the Lord for the ways in which He has intervened to help you in the difficulties of life.

Silence

Listen: "Thus says the LORD, your Redeemer, the Holy One of Israel: 'I am the LORD your God, who teaches you to profit, who leads you by the way you should go. Oh, that you had heeded My commandments! Then your peace would have been like a river, and your righteousness like the waves of the sea'" (Isaiah 48:17-18).

Response: "So that you incline your ear to wisdom, and apply your heart to understanding; yes, if you cry out for discernment, and lift up your voice for understanding, if you seek her as silver, and search for her as for hidden treasures; then you will understand the fear of the LORD, and find the knowledge of God. For the LORD gives wisdom; from His mouth come knowledge and understanding" (Proverbs 2:2-6).

Claim these promises in silence. Ask for and accept the gift of wisdom and discernment for how to pray for others and yourself.

Intercession

Listen: "Let the word of Christ dwell in you richly in all wisdom, teaching and admonishing one another in psalms and hymns and spiritual songs, singing with grace in your hearts to the Lord" (Colossians 3:16).

Response: I will let all bitterness, wrath, anger, clamor and evil speaking be put away from me, with all malice. And I will be kind to others, tenderhearted, forgiving others even as God in Christ forgave me (see Ephesians 4:31-32).

Think of the people you need to forgive and love as you have been forgiven and loved by the Lord. Pray for them!

Supplication

Listen: "If any of you lacks wisdom, let him ask of God, who gives to all liberally and without reproach, and it will be given to him" (James 1:5).

"But the wisdom that is from above is first pure, then peaceable, gentle, willing to yield, full of mercy and good fruits, without partiality and without hypocrisy" (James 3:17).

Response: "As it is written: 'Eye has not seen, nor ear heard, nor have entered into the heart of man the things which God has prepared for those who love Him'" (1 Corinthians 2:9).

Now spread out all your needs before the Lord. Allow Him to show you how to pray and what to pray for in your problems and concerns.

Guidance

Listen: "I have taught you in the way of wisdom; I have led you in right paths" (Proverbs 4:11).

Response: "I will bless the LORD who has given me counsel; my heart also instructs me in the night seasons. I have set the LORD always before me; because He is at my right hand I shall not be moved" (Psalm 16:7-8).

Ask the Lord to guide your decisions today.

Commitment and Empowering

Listen: "Therefore settle it in your hearts not to meditate beforehand on what you will answer; for I will give you a mouth and wisdom which all your adversaries will not be able to contradict or resist" (Luke 21:14-15).

Response: "For the weapons of our warfare are not carnal but mighty in God for pulling down strongholds, casting down arguments and every high thing that exalts itself against the knowledge of God, bringing every thought into captivity to the obedience of Christ" (2 Corinthians 10:4-5).

Now commit to the Lord what He has committed to you. "That good thing which was committed to you, keep by the Holy Spirit who dwells in us" (2 Timothy 1:14).

Day Six

Preparation

Listen: "Come to Me, all you who labor and are heavy laden, and I will give you rest. Take My yoke upon you and learn from Me, for I am gentle and lowly in heart, and you will find rest for your souls. For My yoke is easy and My burden is light" (Matthew 11:28-30).

Response: "For to me, to live is Christ" (Philippians 1:21).

Praise

Listen: "Worthy is the Lamb who was slain to receive power and riches and wisdom, and strength and honor and glory and blessing!" (Revelation 5:12)

Response: "Blessed be the God and Father of our Lord Jesus Christ, who has blessed us with every spiritual blessing in the heavenly places in Christ, just as He chose us in Him before the foundation of the world, that we should be holy and without blame before Him in love, having predestined us to adoption as sons by Jesus Christ to Himself, according to the good pleasure of His will, to the praise of the glory of His grace, by which He has made us accepted in the Beloved" (Ephesians 1:3-6).

Now praise the Lord in your own words with adoration and love.

Confession

Listen: "And the grace of our Lord was exceedingly abundant, with faith and love which are in Christ Jesus. This is a faithful saying and worthy of all acceptance, that Christ Jesus came into the world to save sinners, of whom I am chief " (1 Timothy 1:14-15).

Response: "For there is one God and one Mediator between God and men, the Man Christ Jesus, who gave Himself a ransom for all" (1 Timothy 2:5-6).

Now claim that through the cross you have been forgiven. Accept the forgiveness that is already yours. Allow the Lord to guide you in your confession and listen for His assurance of forgiveness and His power to be free of repetitive patterns of sin and failure.

Thanksgiving

Listen: "For you know the grace of our Lord Jesus Christ, that though He was rich, yet for your sakes He became poor, that you through His poverty might become rich" (2 Corinthians 8:9).

Response: "Thanks be to God for His indescribable gift" (2 Corinthians 9:15).

Pause to thank God for all that is yours through the life, death, resurrection, and indwelling power of Christ.

Silence

Listen: "Come aside by yourselves...and rest a while" (Mark 6:31).

"For without Me you can do nothing" (John 15:5b).

Response: I will let the word of Christ dwell in me richly (see Colossians 3:16).

In the silence, meditate on the wonder that you are destined to be reformed in the image of Christ.

Intercession

Listen: "And I will give you the keys of the kingdom of heaven, and whatever you bind on earth will be bound in heaven, and whatever you loose on earth will be loosed in heaven" (Matthew 16:19).

Response: "Beloved, let us love one another, for love is of God; and everyone who loves is born of God and knows God. He who does not love does not know God, for God is love. In this the love of God was manifested toward us, that God has sent His only begotten Son into the world, that we might live through Him" (1 John 4:7-9).

Now pray specifically for the people in your life to whom you have said, "I'll be praying for you."

Supplication

Listen: "Most assuredly, I say to you, whatever you ask the Father in My name, He will give you. Until now you have asked nothing in My name. Ask, and you will receive, that your joy may be full" (John 16:23-24).

Response: The joy of the Lord is my strength (see Nehemiah 8:10).

Reflect on what robs you of the Lord's joy. Ask the Lord to reveal that to you. Then pray for a fresh infilling of His joy.

Guidance

Listen: "Come now, you who say, 'Today or tomorrow we will go to such and such a city, spend a year there, buy and sell, and make a profit'; whereas you do not know what will happen tomorrow. For what is your life? It is even a vapor that appears for a little time and then vanishes away. Instead, you ought to say, 'If the Lord wills, we shall live and do this or that.' But now you boast in your arrogance. All such boasting is evil. Therefore, to him who knows to do good and does not do it, to him it is sin" (James 4:13-17).

Response: I will rejoice always, pray without ceasing, in everything give thanks; for this is the will of God in Christ Jesus for me (1 Thessalonians 5:16-18).

Now list out the decisions and choices you must make and thank the Lord in advance for His guidance.

Commitment and Empowering

Listen: "I beseech you therefore, brethren, by the mercies of God, that you present your bodies a living sacrifice, holy, acceptable to God, which is your reasonable service. And do not be conformed to this world, but be transformed by the renewing of your mind, that you may prove what is that good and acceptable and perfect will of God" (Romans 12:1-2).

Response: I will not be overcome by evil, but will overcome evil with good (see Romans 12:21).

Now commit yourself anew to the Lord; He is committed to helping you. Because of His greatness, this is going to be a great day!

Day Seven

Preparation

Listen: "Blessed be the God and Father of our Lord Jesus Christ, who according to His abundant mercy has begotten us again to a living hope through the resurrection of Jesus Christ from the dead, to an inheritance incorruptible and undefiled and that does not fade away, reserved in heaven for you" (1 Peter 1:3-4).

Response: In this I greatly rejoice, though now for a little while, if need be, I have been grieved by various trials, that the genuineness of my faith, being much more precious than gold that perishes, though it is tested by fire, may be found to praise, honor, and glory at the revelation of Jesus Christ, whom having not seen I love. Though now, I do not see Him, yet believing, I rejoice with joy inexpressible (see 1 Peter 1:6-8).

Praise

Listen: "But you are a chosen generation, a royal priesthood, a holy nation, His own special people, that you may proclaim the praises of Him who called you out of darkness into His marvelous light" (1 Peter 2:9).

Response: "To Him be the glory and the dominion forever and ever. Amen" (1 Peter 5:11).

Take time now to praise the Lord that He has chosen, called, and elected you to be His beloved and blessed person.

Confession

Listen: "Nevertheless I have this against you, that you have left your first love. Remember therefore from where you have fallen; repent and do the first works, or else I will come to you quickly and remove your lampstand from its place—unless you repent" (Revelation 2:4-5).

Response: I will walk in love, as Christ also has loved me and given Himself for me (see Ephesians 5:2).

Now pause to reflect on what or whom can compete with Christ as your first love. Confess what He shows you may have become your first love in place of Him.

Thanksgiving

Listen: "It is good to give thanks to the LORD, and to sing praises to Your name, O Most High; to declare Your lovingkindness in the morning, and Your faithfulness every night" (Psalm 92:1-2).

Response: "Whom have I in heaven but You? And there is none upon earth that I desire besides You. My flesh and my heart fail; but God is the strength of my heart and my portion forever" (Psalm 73:25-26).

Reflect on this past week. Count your blessings. Name them one by one. Thank the Lord with a grateful heart.

Silence

Listen: "Speak, for Your servant hears" (1 Samuel 3:10).

Response: "With my whole heart I have sought You; oh, let me not wander from Your commandments! Your word I have hidden in my heart, that I might not sin against You" (Psalm 119:10-12).

Life is a relationship—with the Lord, with ourselves, others, the world around us. What does He have to say to you about what He wants you to be and do in these basic relationships?

Intercession

Listen: "Is anyone among you suffering? Let him pray. Is anyone cheerful? Let him sing psalms. Is anyone among you sick? Let him call for the elders of the church, and let them pray over him with oil in the name of the Lord. And the prayer of faith will save the sick, and the Lord will raise him up. And if he has committed sins, he will be forgiven" (James 5:13-15).

Response: "Now may the God of patience and comfort grant you to be like-minded toward one another, according to Christ Jesus, that you may with one mind and one mouth glorify the God and Father of our Lord Jesus Christ" (Romans 15:5-6).

Now take time to pray for the people on your prayer list. Ask the Lord to guide you in your prayers and then intercede with boldness.

Supplication

Listen: "Seeing then that we have a great High Priest who has passed through the heavens, Jesus the Son of God, let us hold fast our confession. For we do not have a High Priest who cannot sympathize with our weaknesses, but was in all points tempted as we are, yet without sin" (Hebrews 4:14-15).

Response: "Let us therefore come boldly to the throne of grace, that we may obtain mercy and find grace to help in time of need" (Hebrews 4:16).

Tell the Lord what's on your heart as a friend would speak with a friend. He cares about what concerns you!

Guidance

Listen: "The LORD is my shepherd; I shall not want. He makes me to lie down in green pastures; He leads me beside the still waters. He restores my soul; He leads me in the paths of righteousness for His name's sake. Yea, though I walk through the valley of the shadow of death, I will fear no evil; for You are with me; Your rod and Your staff, they comfort me. You prepare a table before me in the presence of my enemies; You anoint my head with oil; my cup runs over. Surely goodness and mercy shall follow me all the days of my life; and I will dwell in the house of the LORD forever" (Psalm 23).

Response: "Know that the LORD, He is God; it is He who has made us, and not we ourselves; we are His people and the sheep of His pasture" (Psalm 100:3).

Now give the Lord control of your mind to think His thoughts. He created you to know and do His will.

Commitment and Empowering

Listen: "You did not choose Me, but I chose you and appointed you that you should go and bear fruit, and that your fruit should remain, that whatever you ask the Father in My name He may give you" (John 15:16).

Response: "Also I heard the voice of the Lord, saying: 'Whom shall I send, and who will go for Us?' Then I said, 'Here am I! Send me'" (Isaiah 6:8).

May the Lord go before me to show the way, behind me to encourage me, beside me to befriend me, above me to watch over me, and within me to give me power!

Day Eight

Preparation

Listen: "Behold, I stand at the door and knock. If anyone hears My voice and opens the door, I will come in to him and dine with him, and he with Me" (Revelation 3:20).

Response: If I confess with my mouth the Lord Jesus, and believe in my heart that God has raised Him from the dead, I will be saved. For with the heart I believe...and with my mouth my confession is made to salvation (see Romans 10:9-10).

Praise

Listen: "For you did not receive the spirit of bondage again to fear, but you received the Spirit of adoption by whom we cry out, 'Abba, Father' " (Romans 8:15).

Response: "The Spirit Himself bears witness with our spirit that we are children of God, and if children, then heirs— heirs of God and joint heirs with Christ, if indeed we suffer with Him, that we may also be glorified together" (Romans 8:16-17).

Praise is the thermostat of our souls. When we praise the Lord for who He is, our minds and hearts are opened to receive the inflow of His Spirit. Praise the Lord! Allow your whole being to soar in adoration.

Confession

Listen: "But He was wounded for our transgressions, He was bruised for our iniquities; the chastisement for our peace was upon Him, and by His stripes we are healed. All we like sheep have gone astray; we have turned, every one, to his own way; and the Lord has laid on Him the iniquity of us all" (Isaiah 53:5-6).

Response: "And you, being dead in your trespasses and the uncircumcision of your flesh, He has made alive together with Him, having forgiven you all trespasses, having wiped out the handwriting of requirements that was against us, which was contrary to us. And He has taken it out of the way, having nailed it to the cross" (Colossians 2:13-14).

Now nail to the cross your sins and failures and claim forgiveness and power to begin again.

Thanksgiving

Listen: "As you have therefore received Christ Jesus the Lord, so walk in Him, rooted and built up in Him and established in the faith, as you have been taught, abounding in it with thanksgiving" (Colossians 2:6-7).

Response: "And I thank Christ Jesus our Lord who has enabled me" (1 Timothy 1:12).

Now thank the Lord for His goodness and love.

Silence

Listen: "If then you were raised with Christ, seek those things which are above, where Christ is, sitting at the right hand of God. Set your mind on things above, not on things on the earth. For you died, and your life is hidden with Christ in God. When Christ who is our life appears, then you also will appear with Him in glory" (Colossians 3:1-4).

Response: "But now you must also put off all these: anger, wrath, malice, blasphemy, filthy language out of your mouth. Do not lie to one another, since you have put off the old man with his deeds, and have put on the new man who is renewed in knowledge according to the image of Him who created him, where there is neither Greek nor Jew, circumcised nor uncircumcised, barbarian, Scythian, slave nor free, but Christ is all and in all" (Colossians 3:8-11).

Allow the Lord to reveal to you any inner thoughts or motives that need to be changed.

Intercession

Listen: "Therefore, as the elect of God, holy and beloved, put on tender mercies, kindness, humility, meekness, long-suffering; bearing with one another, and forgiving one another, if anyone has a complaint against another; even as Christ forgave you, so you also must do. But above all these things put on love, which is the bond of perfection" (Colossians 3:12-14).

Response: "And let the peace of God rule in your hearts, to which also you were called in one body; and be thankful. Let the word of Christ dwell in you richly in all wisdom, teaching and admonishing one another in psalms and hymns and spiritual songs, singing with grace in your hearts to the Lord. And whatever you do in word or deed, do all in the name of the Lord Jesus, giving thanks to God the Father through Him" (Colossians 3:15-17).

Pray specifically for loved ones, friends, people with whom you work, neighbors, those in government, leaders in the church, and those with special needs today.

Supplication

Listen:　"Continue earnestly in prayer, being vigilant in it with thanksgiving; meanwhile praying also for us, that God would open to us a door for the word, to speak the mystery of Christ, for which I am also in chains, that I may make it manifest, as I ought to speak" (Colossians 4:2-4).

Response:　"Walk in wisdom toward those who are outside, redeeming the time. Let your speech always be with grace, seasoned with salt, that you may know how you ought to answer each one" (Colossians 4:5-6).

Pause to think and pray about those you know who need Christ and your personal witness of what He means to you.

Guidance

Listen:　"And of His fullness we have all received, and grace for grace. For the law was given through Moses, but grace and truth came through Jesus Christ" (John 1:16).

Response:　"Let us therefore come boldly to the throne of grace, that we may obtain mercy and find grace to help in time of need" (Hebrews 4:16).

Give the Lord lead time to guide you in future decisions. Ask Him to reveal His will for His best in your life.

Commitment and Empowering

Listen:　"All things are yours...the world or life or death, or things present or things to come—all are yours, and you are Christ's and Christ is God's" (see 1 Corinthians 3:21-23).

Response: May I be known as a servant of Christ and a steward of the mysteries of God (see 1 Corinthians 4:1).

Now commit to the Lord this day and all that is ahead of you. He wants to help you have a joyous day!

Day Nine

Preparation

Listen: "'For I know the thoughts that I think toward you,' says the LORD, 'thoughts of peace and not of evil, to give you a future and a hope. Then you will call upon Me and go and pray to Me, and I will listen to you. And you will seek Me and find Me, when you search for Me with all your heart. I will be found by you,' says the LORD" (Jeremiah 29:11-14a).

Response: "For in You, O LORD, I hope; You will hear, O Lord my God" (Psalm 38:15).

Praise

Listen: "But I will hope continually, and will praise You yet more and more. My mouth shall tell of Your righteousness and Your salvation all the day, for I do not know their limits. I will go in the strength of the Lord GOD; I will make mention of Your righteousness, of Yours only" (Psalm 71:14-16).

Response: "Happy is he who has the God of Jacob for his help, whose hope is in the LORD his God" (Psalm 146:5).

Praise is the antidote for pride. Praise the Lord for choosing to be your God and for choosing you to know, love, and serve Him.

Confession

Listen: "As far as the east is from the west, so far has He removed our transgressions from us" (Psalm 103:12).

Response: "This hope we have as an anchor of the soul, both sure and steadfast, and which enters the Presence behind the veil" (Hebrews 6:19).

Now ask the Lord to guide your confession.

Thanksgiving

Listen: "I wait for the LORD, my soul waits, and in His word I do hope" (Psalm 130:5).

Response: "The LORD takes pleasure in those who fear Him, in those who hope in His mercy" (Psalm 147:11).

Think of what life would be without the Lord's blessings. Then thank Him for all He has done for you.

Silence

Listen: "Truly my soul waits silently for God; from Him comes my salvation....My soul, wait silently for God alone, for my expectation is from Him. He only is my rock and my salvation" (Psalm 62:1,5-6).

Response: "Now faith is the substance of things hoped for, the evidence of things not seen" (Hebrews 11:1).

In silence, listen to the Lord as He reveals to you that He is more ready to give than you may be ready to ask. Silence prepares us for our intercession and supplication. Listen!

Intercession

Listen: "For what is our hope, or joy, or crown of rejoicing? Is it not even you in the presence of our Lord Jesus Christ at His coming?" (1 Thessalonians 2:19).

Response: "Love suffers long and is kind; love does not envy; love does not parade itself, is not puffed up; does not behave rudely, does not seek its own, is not provoked, thinks no evil; does not rejoice in iniquity, but rejoices in the truth; bears all things, believes all things, hopes all things, endures all things. Love never fails" (1 Corinthians 13:4-8a).

Now pray for the power to love in this magnificent, creative way.

Supplication

Listen: "Behold what manner of love the Father has bestowed on us, that we should be called children of God! Therefore the world does not know us, because it did not know Him. Beloved, now we are children of God; and it has not yet been revealed what we shall be, but we know that when He is revealed, we shall be like Him, for we shall see Him as He is" (1 John 3:1-2).

Response: "Therefore gird up the loins of your mind, be sober, and rest your hope fully upon the grace that is to be brought to you at the revelation of Jesus Christ" (1 Peter 1:13).

The Lord has serendipities in store for us, surprises of His grace. Trust all of your needs to Him; He is at work in your life.

Guidance

Listen: "The Lord will guide you continually, and satisfy your soul in drought, and strengthen your bones; you shall be like a watered garden, and like a spring of water, whose waters do not fail" (Isaiah 58:11).

Response: "For You are my rock and my fortress; therefore, for Your name's sake, lead me and guide me" (Psalm 31:3).

Ask the Lord to prepare you for decisions and choices ahead. He will prepare you for what He has prepared.

Commitment and Empowering

Listen: "Now may the God of hope fill you with all joy and peace in believing, that you may abound in hope by the power of the Holy Spirit" (Romans 15:13).

Response: "And God is able to make all grace abound toward you, that you, always having all sufficiency in all things, may have an abundance for every good work" (2 Corinthians 9:8).

"I have hope!" (Acts 24:15)

Live today expectantly. The Lord has plans for you, for your growth and His glory!

Day Ten

Preparation

Listen: "But My faithfulness and My mercy shall be with him" (Psalm 89:24).

Response: "This is a faithful saying: For if we die with Him, we shall also live with Him. If we endure, we shall also reign with Him. If we deny Him, He also will deny us. If we are faithless, He remains faithful; He cannot deny Himself " (2 Timothy 2:11-13).

Praise

Listen: "[The Lord's mercies] are new every morning; great is Your faithfulness" (Lamentations 3:23).

Response: "I will sing of the mercies of the LORD forever; with my mouth will I make known Your faithfulness to all generations" (Psalm 89:1).

Now praise the Lord for His daily mercies in your life and for His consistent faithfulness.

Confession

Listen: "If we confess our sins, He is faithful and just to forgive us our sins and to cleanse us from all unrighteousness" (1 John 1:9).

Response: "No temptation has overtaken you except such as is common to man; but God is faithful, who will not allow you to be tempted beyond what you are able, but with the temptation will also make the way of escape, that you may be able to bear it" (1 Corinthians 10:13).

Now confess the temptations you face and thank the Lord for giving you the power to overcome them.

Thanksgiving

Listen: "Enter into His gates with thanksgiving, and into His courts with praise. Be thankful to Him and bless His name. For the LORD is good; His mercy is everlasting, and His truth endures to all generations" (Psalm 100:4-5).

"So you shall rejoice in every good thing which the LORD your God has given to you" (Deuteronomy 26:11).

Response: To Him who loved me and washed me from my sins in His own blood, and has made me a king and priest to His God and Father, to Him be glory and dominion forever and ever. Amen (see Revelation 1:5-6).

Now count your blessings and thank the Lord.

Silence

Listen: "Even to your old age, I am He, and even to gray hairs I will carry you! I have made, and I will bear; even I will carry, and will deliver you" (Isaiah 46:4).

Response: I will cast my burden on the Lord, and He shall sustain me (see Psalm 55:22).

Now in silence trust your burdens to the Lord.

Intercession

Listen: "Now may our Lord Jesus Christ Himself, and our God and Father, who has loved us and given us everlasting consolation and good hope by grace, comfort your hearts and establish you in every good word and work" (2 Thessalonians 2:16-17).

Response: "Finally, brethren, pray for us, that the word of the Lord may run swiftly and be glorified, just as it is with you, and that we may be delivered from unreasonable and wicked men; for not all have faith" (2 Thessalonians 3:1-2).

Now pray for the problems people face living out their faith. Name people and their challenges specifically.

Supplication

Listen: "Let, I pray, Your merciful kindness be for my comfort, according to Your word to Your servant. Let Your tender mercies come to me, that I may live; for Your law is my delight" (Psalm 119:76-77).

Response: "Hear my prayer, O LORD, give ear to my supplications! In Your faithfulness answer me, and in Your righteousness" (Psalm 143:1).

Now claim the Lord's faithfulness in your needs.

Guidance

Listen: "His lord said to him, 'Well done, good and faithful servant; you were faithful over a few things, I will make you ruler over many things. Enter into the joy of your lord.' He also who had received two talents came and said, 'Lord, you delivered to me two talents; look, I have gained two more talents besides them.' His lord said to him, 'Well done, good and faithful servant; you were faithful over a few things, I will make you ruler over many things. Enter into the joy of your lord'" (Matthew 25:21-23).

Response: I pray that I may be steadfast, immovable, always abounding in the work of the Lord, knowing that my labor is not in vain in the Lord (see 1 Corinthians 15:58).

Thank the Lord in advance for His guidance in all of the opportunities of this day.

Commitment and Empowering

Listen: "Now may the God of peace Himself sanctify you completely; and may your whole spirit, soul, and body be preserved blameless at the coming of our Lord Jesus Christ. He who calls you is faithful, who also will do it" (1 Thessalonians 5:23-24).

Response: Whatever I do, may I do all to Your glory, O God (see 1 Corinthians 10:31).

This is the day to glorify the Lord!

Day Eleven

Preparation

Listen: "If you abide in Me, and My words abide in you, you will ask what you desire, and it shall be done for you. By this My Father is glorified, that you bear much fruit; so you will be My disciples. As the Father loved Me, I also have loved you; abide in My love. If you keep My commandments, you will abide in My love, just as I have kept My Father's commandments and abide in His love. These things I have spoken to you, that My joy may remain in you, and that your joy may be full" (John 15:7-11).

Response: "The joy of the LORD is your strength" (Nehemiah 8:10).

Praise

Listen: "Therefore you now have sorrow; but I will see you again and your heart will rejoice, and your joy no one will take from you" (John 16:22).

Response: "You have made known to me the ways of life; You will make me full of joy in Your presence" (Acts 2:28).

Now pause to praise the Lord for the joy He gives to your life.

Confession

Listen: "Looking unto Jesus, the author and finisher of our faith, who for the joy that was set before Him endured the cross, despising the shame, and has sat down at the right hand of the throne of God" (Hebrews 12:2).

Response: "Restore to me the joy of Your salvation, and uphold me by Your generous Spirit" (Psalm 51:12).

Now confess whatever the Lord brings to mind that needs His cleansing forgiveness.

Thanksgiving

Listen: "Yet I will rejoice in the LORD, I will joy in the God of my salvation. The LORD God is my strength; He will make my feet like deer's feet, and He will make me walk on my high hills" (Habakkuk 3:18-19).

Response: "Oh come, let us sing to the LORD! Let us shout joyfully to the Rock of our salvation. Let us come before His presence with thanksgiving; let us shout joyfully to Him with psalms" (Psalm 95:1-2).

Take time to thank the Lord for His constant faithfulness.

Silence

Listen: "Now may the God of hope fill you with all joy and peace in believing, that you may abound in hope by the power of the Holy Spirit" (Romans 15:13).

Response: "I will greatly rejoice in the LORD, my soul shall be joyful in my God; for He has clothed me with the garments of salvation, He has covered me with the robe of righteousness, as a bridegroom decks himself with ornaments, and as a bride adorns herself with her jewels" (Isaiah 61:10).

In silence, allow the Lord to help you picture yourself filled with His joy.

Intercession

Listen: "That which was from the beginning, which we have heard, which we have seen with our eyes, which we have looked upon, and our hands have handled, concerning the Word of life—the life was manifested, and we have seen, and bear witness and declare to you that eternal life which was with the Father and was manifested to us—that which we have seen and heard we declare to you, that you also may have fellowship with us; and truly our fellowship is with the Father and with His Son Jesus Christ. And these things we write to you that your joy may be full" (1 John 1:1-4).

Response: "For this reason we also, since the day we heard it, do not cease to pray for you, and to ask that you may be filled with the knowledge of His will in all wisdom and spiritual understanding; that you may have a walk worthy of the Lord, fully pleasing Him, being fruitful in every good work and increasing in the knowledge of God; strengthened with all might, according to His glorious power, for all patience and longsuffering with joy" (Colossians 1:9-11).

Now claim your authority to intercede for loved ones, friends, and others. Today, claim for them this awesome promise.

Supplication

Listen: "Until now you have asked nothing in My name. Ask, and you will receive, that your joy may be full" (John 16:24).

Response: "That I may finish my race with joy" (Acts 20:24).

Now turn over to the Lord the needs of your life in which you need to experience and express joy.

Guidance

Listen: "The kingdom of God is...righteousness and peace and joy in the Holy Spirit" (Romans 14:17).

Response: "I delight to do Your will, O my God, and Your law is within my heart" (Psalm 40:8).

Ask the Lord to guide you in all you do and say this day.

Commitment and Empowering

Listen: "Commit your way to the LORD, trust also in Him, and He shall bring it to pass....Rest in the LORD, and wait patiently for Him" (Psalm 37:5,7).

Response: "One thing I do, forgetting those things which are behind and reaching forward to those things which are ahead, I press toward the goal for the prize of the upward call of God in Christ Jesus" (Philippians 3:13-14).

Joy is the sure sign that Christ lives in us. This is a day to live with joy!

Day Twelve

Preparation

Listen: "Peace I leave with you, My peace I give to you; not as the world gives do I give to you. Let not your heart be troubled, neither let it be afraid" (John 14:27).

Response: I will let the peace of God rule in my heart...and let the word of Christ dwell in me richly in all wisdom (see Colossians 3:15-16).

Praise

Listen: "Therefore, having been justified by faith, we have peace with God through our Lord Jesus Christ" (Romans 5:1).

Response: "Mercy and truth have met together; righteousness and peace have kissed" (Psalm 85:10).

Now praise the Lord for His peace.

Confession

Listen: "Grace to you and peace from God the Father and our Lord Jesus Christ, who gave Himself for our sins, that He might deliver us from this present evil age, according to the will of our God and Father" (Galatians 1:3-4).

Response: For it pleased You, Father, that in Him all the fullness should dwell, and by Him to reconcile all things to Himself, by Him, whether things on earth or in heaven, having made peace by the blood of the cross. And I, who once was alienated and an enemy in my mind by wicked works, yet now He has reconciled (see Colossians 1:19-21).

Now confess those things that keep you from living in the Lord's peace. True peace is the result of knowing we are loved and forgiven.

Thanksgiving

Listen: "Therefore by Him let us continually offer the sacrifice of praise to God, that is, the fruit of our lips, giving thanks to His name" (Hebrews 13:15).

Response: "Oh, give thanks to the LORD, for He is good! For His mercy endures forever. Let the redeemed of the LORD say so" (Psalm 107:1-2).

Reflect on the peace of Christ and give thanks for His peace in the midst of the conflict and frustrations of life.

Silence

Listen: "Peace, be still" (Mark 4:39).

Response: "Finally, brethren, whatever things are true, whatever things are noble, whatever things are just, whatever things are pure, whatever things are lovely, whatever things are of good report, if there is any virtue and if there is anything praiseworthy—meditate on these things. The things which you learned and received and heard and saw in me, these do, and the God of peace will be with you" (Philippians 4:8-9).

Ask the Lord to reveal anything that robs you of His peace.

Intercession

Listen: "For He Himself is our peace, who has made both one, and has broken down the middle wall of separation between us" (Ephesians 2:14).

Response: I will not grieve the Holy Spirit of God, by whom I was sealed for the day of redemption. I will let all bitterness, wrath, anger, clamor, and evil speaking to be put away from me, with all malice. I will be kind to others, tenderhearted, forgiving, just as God in Christ forgave me (see Ephesians 4:30-31).

Now pray for true peace in your relationships.

Supplication

Listen: "Therefore let us pursue the things which make for peace and the things by which one may edify another" (Romans 14:19).

Response: May the Lord of peace Himself give me peace always in every way (see 2 Thessalonians 3:16).

Pray for the Lord's peace as you live with the pressures of life.

Guidance

Listen: "Pursue peace with all people, and holiness, without which no one will see the Lord" (Hebrews 12:14).

Response: Now may the God of peace who brought up our Lord Jesus from the dead, that great Shepherd of the sheep, through the blood of the everlasting covenant, make me complete in every good work to do His will, working in me what is well pleasing in His sight, through Jesus Christ, to whom be glory forever and ever. Amen (see Hebrews 13:20-21).

Seek the Lord's guidance to do and say those things that will reflect His peace.

Commitment and Empowering

Listen: "These things I have spoken to you, that in Me you may have peace. In the world you will have tribulation; but be of good cheer, I have overcome the world" (John 16:33).

"Blessed are the peacemakers, for they shall be called the sons of God" (Matthew 5:9).

"Seek the peace of the city where you dwell, for in its peace you will find your peace" (Jeremiah 29:7 RSV).

Response: "Now may the God of peace Himself sanctify you completely; and may your whole spirit, soul and body be preserved blameless at the coming of our Lord Jesus Christ. He who calls you is faithful, who also will do it" (1 Thessalonians 5:23-24).

Today is a gift of the Lord. Live it to the fullest!

Day Thirteen

Preparation

Listen: "Then He said to them all, 'If anyone desires to come after Me, let him deny himself, and take up his cross daily, and follow Me. For whoever desires to save his life will lose it, but whoever loses his life for My sake will save it. For what profit is it to a man if he gains the whole world, and is himself destroyed or lost? For whoever is ashamed of Me and My words, of him the Son of Man will be ashamed when He comes in His own glory, and in His Father's, and of the holy angels' " (Luke 9:23-26).

Response: "I have been crucified with Christ; it is no longer I who live, but Christ lives in me; and the life which I now live in the flesh I live by faith in the Son of God, who loved me and gave Himself for me" (Galatians 2:20).

Praise

Listen: "How beautiful upon the mountains are the feet of him who brings good news, who proclaims peace, who brings glad tidings of good things, who proclaims salvation, who says to Zion, 'Your God reigns!' " (Isaiah 52:7).

Response: "For with You is the fountain of life; in Your light we see light" (Psalm 36:9).

Now express to the Lord the praise of your heart.

Confession

Listen: "And whenever you stand praying, if you have anything against anyone, forgive him, that your Father in heaven may also forgive you your trespasses. But if you do not forgive, neither will your Father in heaven forgive your trespasses" (Mark 11:25-26).

Response: "But God forbid that I should boast except in the cross of our Lord Jesus Christ, by whom the world has been crucified to me, and I to the world. For in Christ Jesus neither circumcision nor uncircumcision avails anything, but a new creation" (Galatians 6:14-15).

Allow the Lord to guide your confession and show you what needs to be confessed and forgiven.

Thanksgiving

Listen: "Give unto the LORD the glory due to His name; worship the LORD in the beauty of holiness" (Psalm 29:2).

Response: "Now thanks be to God who always leads us in triumph in Christ, and through us diffuses the fragrance of His knowledge in every place" (2 Corinthians 2:14).

Think of the ways Christ has enabled you to triumph in trouble and give thanks with a grateful heart.

Silence

Listen: "Wait on the LORD; be of good courage, and He shall strengthen your heart; wait, I say, on the LORD" (Psalm 27:14).

Response: "I wait for the LORD, my soul waits, and in His word I do hope. My soul waits for the Lord" (Psalm 130:5-6).

Now claim the wonder that the Lord will communicate His grace, guidance, and goodness as you wait for Him in silence.

Intercession

Listen: "But you, beloved, building yourselves up on your most holy faith, praying in the Holy Spirit, keep yourselves in the love of God, looking for the mercy of our Lord Jesus Christ unto eternal life" (Jude 20-21).

Response: "I thank my God, making mention of you always in my prayers, hearing of your love and faith which you have toward the Lord Jesus and toward all the saints, that the sharing of your faith may become effective by the acknowledgment of every good thing which is in you in Christ Jesus" (Philemon 4-6).

Now intercede for the people in your life and those with special needs.

Supplication

Listen: "My grace is sufficient for you, for My strength is made perfect in weakness" (2 Corinthians 12:9a).

Response: "Therefore most gladly I will rather boast in my infirmities, that the power of Christ may rest upon me. Therefore I take pleasure in infirmities, in reproaches, in needs, in persecutions, in distresses, for Christ's sake. For when I am weak, then I am strong" (2 Corinthians 12:9b-10).

Ask for the Lord's power for any pain or suffering you are experiencing.

Guidance

Listen: "Let this mind be in you which was also in Christ Jesus, who, being in the form of God, did not consider it robbery to be equal with God, but made Himself of no reputation, taking the form of a bondservant, and coming in the likeness of men. And being found in appearance as a man, He humbled Himself and became obedient to the point of death, even the death of the cross. Therefore God also has highly exalted Him and given Him the name which is above every name, that at the name of Jesus every knee should bow, of those in heaven, and of those on earth, and of those under the earth, and that every tongue should confess that Jesus Christ is Lord, to the glory of God the Father" (Philippians 2:5-11).

Response: "Yet indeed I also count all things loss for the excellence of the knowledge of Christ Jesus my Lord, for whom I have suffered the loss of all things, and count them as rubbish, that I may gain Christ and be found in Him, not having my own righteousness, which is from the law, but that which is through faith in Christ, the righteousness which is from God by faith; that I may know Him and the power of His resurrection, and the fellowship of His sufferings, being conformed to His death, if, by any means, I may attain to the resurrection from the dead. Not that I have already attained, or am already perfected; but I press on, that I may lay hold of that for which Christ Jesus has also laid hold of me" (Philippians 3:8-12).

Now trust your decisions and plans to the Lord's guidance.

Commitment and Empowering

Listen: "Finally, my brethren, be strong in the Lord and in the power of His might. Put on the whole armor of God, that you may be able to stand against the wiles of the devil. For we do not wrestle against flesh and blood, but against principalities, against powers, against the rulers of the darkness of this age, against spiritual hosts of wickedness in the heavenly places. Therefore take up the whole armor of God, that you may be able to withstand in the evil day, and having done all, to stand.

"Stand therefore, having girded your waist with truth, having put on the breastplate of righteousness, and having shod your feet with the preparation of the gospel of peace; above all, taking the shield of faith with which you will be able to quench all the fiery darts of the wicked one. And take the helmet of salvation, and the sword of the Spirit, which is the word of God; praying always with all prayer and supplication in the Spirit, being watchful to this end with all perseverance and supplication for all the saints" (Ephesians 6:10-18).

Response: "And this is the victory that has overcome the world— our faith. Who is he who overcomes the world, but he who believes that Jesus is the Son of God?" (1 John 5:4-5).

As a believer in Jesus, the Son of God, commit the day to Him.

Day Fourteen

Preparation

Listen: "Most assuredly, I say to you, he who hears My word and believes in Him who sent Me has everlasting life, and shall not come into judgment, but has passed from death into life" (John 5:24).

Response: "Beloved, if our heart does not condemn us, we have confidence toward God. And whatever we ask we receive from Him, because we keep His commandments and do those things that are pleasing in His sight. And this is His commandment: that we should believe on the name of His Son Jesus Christ and love one another, as He gave us commandment. Now he who keeps His commandments abides in Him, and He in him. And by this we know that He abides in us, by the Spirit whom He has given us" (1 John 3:21-24).

Praise

Listen: "And we have such trust through Christ toward God" (2 Corinthians 3:4).

Response: "It is better to trust in the LORD than to put confidence in man. It is better to trust in the LORD than to put confidence in princes" (Psalm 118:8-9).

Now praise the Lord for Himself in your own words of adoration.

Confession

Listen: "Blessed is he whose transgression is forgiven, whose sin is covered. Blessed is the man to whom the LORD does not impute iniquity, and in whose spirit there is no deceit. When I kept silent, my bones grew old through my groaning all the day long. For day and night Your hand was heavy upon me; my vitality was turned into the drought of summer" (Psalm 32:1-4).

Response: "I acknowledged my sin to You, and my iniquity I have not hidden. I said, 'I will confess my transgressions to the LORD,' and You forgave the iniquity of my sin" (Psalm 32:5).

Now confess whatever the Lord has shown you that needs His forgiveness.

Thanksgiving

Listen: "Now He who has prepared us for this very thing is God, who also has given us the Spirit as a guarantee. So we are always confident, knowing that while we are at home in the body we are absent from the Lord" (2 Corinthians 5:5-6).

Response: "For we walk by faith, not by sight. We are confident, yes, well pleased rather to be absent from the body and to be present with the Lord" (2 Corinthians 5:7-8).

Now list out in your mind the blessings of God for which you are thankful today, and thank Him with a grateful heart.

Silence

Listen: "For thus says the Lord GOD, the Holy One of Israel:

'In returning and rest you shall be saved; in quietness and confidence shall be your strength'" (Isaiah 30:15).

Response: "By awesome deeds in righteousness You will answer us, O God of our salvation, You who are the confidence of all the ends of the earth, and of the far-off seas" (Psalm 65:5).

Now be silent and listen as you meditate. Ask the Lord to guide your reflection on the needs of others, and what He has to say about what He wants you to be and do.

Intercession

Listen: "Now this is the confidence that we have in Him, that if we ask anything according to His will, He hears us" (1 John 5:14).

Response: "And if we know that He hears us, whatever we ask, we know that we have the petitions that we have asked of Him" (1 John 5:15).

Now intercede for family, friends, people in special need, and the sick.

Supplication

Listen: "You are an epistle of Christ, ministered by us, written not with ink but by the Spirit of the living God, not on tablets of stone but on tablets of flesh, that is, of the heart. And we have such trust through Christ toward God" (2 Corinthians 3:3-4).

Response: "Not that we are sufficient of ourselves to think of anything as being from ourselves, but our sufficiency is from God" (2 Corinthians 3:5).

Now pray for specific responsibilities and relationships in which you need guidance.

Guidance

Listen: "Now the Lord spoke to Paul in the night by a vision, 'Do not be afraid, but speak, and do not keep silent; for I am with you, and no one will attack you to hurt you; for I have many people in this city'" (Acts 18:9).

Response: "Therefore, King Agrippa, I was not disobedient to the heavenly vision" (Acts 26:19).

Commitment and Empowering

Listen: "I beseech you therefore, brethren, by the mercies of God, that you present your bodies a living sacrifice, holy, acceptable to God, which is your reasonable service" (Romans 12:1).

Response: I will not be conformed to this world, but I will be transformed by the renewing of my mind, that I may prove what is that good and acceptable and perfect will of God (see Romans 12:2).

Now commit your life anew, surrender the needs of the day ahead, and trust the Lord completely.

Day Fifteen

Preparation

Listen: "I am the resurrection and the life. He who believes in Me, though he may die, he shall live" (John 11:25).

Response: Yes, Lord, I believe You are the Christ, the Son of the living God (see John 11:27).

Praise

Listen: "He is not here, but is risen! Remember how He spoke to you when He was still in Galilee, saying, 'The Son of Man must be delivered into the hands of sinful men, and be crucified, and the third day rise again.' And they remembered His words" (Luke 24:6-8).

Response: Christ is risen! He is risen indeed.

Praise the risen Christ for His victory over death, His triumphant power with you, and His liberating power in you. Make today a celebration of the resurrection.

Confession

Listen: "What shall we say then? Shall we continue in sin that grace may abound? Certainly not! How shall we who died to sin live any longer in it? Or do you not know that as many of us as were baptized into Christ

Jesus were baptized into His death? Therefore we were buried with Him through baptism into death, that just as Christ was raised from the dead by the glory of the Father, even so we also should walk in newness of life.

"For if we have been united together in the likeness of His death, certainly we also shall be in the likeness of His resurrection, knowing this, that our old man was crucified with Him, that the body of sin might be done away with, that we should no longer be slaves of sin. For he who has died has been freed from sin" (Romans 6:1-7).

Response: "Now if we died with Christ, we believe that we shall also live with Him, knowing that Christ, having been raised from the dead, dies no more. Death no longer has dominion over Him. For the death that He died, He died to sin once for all; but the life that He lives, He lives to God. Likewise you also, reckon yourselves to be dead indeed to sin, but alive to God in Christ Jesus our Lord.

"Therefore do not let sin reign in your mortal body, that you should obey it in its lusts. And do not present your members as instruments of unrighteousness to sin, but present yourselves to God as being alive from the dead, and your members as instruments of righteousness to God. For sin shall not have dominion over you, for you are not under law but under grace" (Romans 6:8-14).

With this assurance, make your confession to the Lord.

Thanksgiving

Listen: "So when this corruptible has put on incorruption, and this mortal has put on immortality, then shall be brought to pass the saying that is written: 'Death is swallowed up in victory. O Death, where is your sting? O Hades, where is your victory?'" (1 Corinthians 15:54-55).

Response: "The sting of death is sin, and the strength of sin is the law. But thanks be to God, who gives us the victory through our Lord Jesus Christ. Therefore, my beloved brethren, be steadfast, immovable, always abounding in the work of the Lord, knowing that your labor is not in vain in the Lord" (1 Corinthians 15:56-58).

Silence

Listen: "And when I saw Him, I fell at His feet as dead. But He laid His right hand to me, saying to me, 'Do not be afraid; I am the First and the Last. I am He who lives, and was dead, and behold, I am alive forevermore. Amen. And I have the keys of Hades and of Death'" (Revelation 1:17-18).

Response: *In the silence, sense the hand of the risen Christ upon you and claim His victorious power in your life.*

Intercession

Listen: "Now may the God of peace who brought up our Lord Jesus from the dead, that great Shepherd of the sheep, through the blood of the everlasting covenant, make you complete in every good work to do His will, working in you what is well pleasing in His sight, through Jesus Christ, to whom be glory forever and ever. Amen" (Hebrews 13:20-21).

Response: "Therefore we do not lose heart. Even though our outward man is perishing, yet the inward man is being renewed day by day. For our light affliction, which is but for a moment, is working for us a far more exceeding and eternal weight of glory, while we do not look at the things which are seen, but at the things which are not seen. For the things which are seen are temporary, but the things which are not seen are eternal" (2 Corinthians 4:16-18).

Now pray for the needs of others.

Supplication

Listen: "That I may know Him and the power of His resurrection, and the fellowship of His sufferings, being conformed to His death, if, by any means, I may attain to the resurrection from the dead" (Philippians 3:10-11).

Response: "Not that I have already attained, or am already perfected; but I press on, that I may lay hold of that for which Christ Jesus has also laid hold of me. Brethren, I do not count myself to have apprehended; but one thing I do, forgetting those things which are behind and reaching forward to those things which are ahead, I press toward the goal for the prize of the upward call of God in Christ Jesus" (Philippians 3:12-14).

Is Paul's magnificent, liberating obsession the passion of my life? How would I live today if it were?

Guidance

Listen: "But God, who is rich in mercy, because of His great love with which He loved us, even when we were dead in trespasses, made us alive together with Christ (by grace you have been saved), and raised us up together, and made us sit together in the heavenly places in Christ Jesus, that in the ages to come He might show the exceeding riches of His grace in His kindness toward us in Christ Jesus" (Ephesians 2:4-7).

Response: For by grace I have been saved through faith, and that not of myself; it is the gift of God, not of works, lest I should boast (see Ephesians 2:8-9).

Commitment and Empowering

Listen: "And Jesus came and spoke to them, saying, 'All authority has been given to Me in heaven and on earth. Go therefore and make disciples of all the nations, baptizing them in the name of the Father and of the Son and of the Holy Spirit, teaching them to observe all things that I have commanded you; and lo, I am with you always, even to the end of the age'" (Matthew 28:18-20).

Response: Amen.

Day Sixteen

Preparation

Listen: "Behold, I send the Promise of My Father upon you; but tarry in the city of Jerusalem until you are endued with power from on high" (Luke 24:49).

Response: "This Jesus God has raised up, of which we are all witnesses. Therefore being exalted to the right hand of God, and having received from the Father the promise of the Holy Spirit, He poured out this which you now see and hear" (Acts 2:32-33).

Praise

Listen: "If anyone thirsts, let him come to Me and drink. He who believes in Me as the Scripture has said, out of his heart will flow rivers of living water" (John 7:37-38).

Response: "By this we know that we abide in Him, and He in us, because He has given us of His Spirit. And we have seen and testify that the Father has sent the Son as Savior of the world. Whoever confesses that Jesus is the Son of God, God abides in him, and he in God" (1 John 4:13-15).

Take time to praise the Lord for the gift of the Holy Spirit and the rivers of living water flowing in your life.

Confession

Listen: "Do not grieve the Holy Spirit" (Ephesians 4:30).

"Do not quench the Spirit" (1 Thessalonians 5:19).

"Be filled with the Spirit" (Ephesians 5:18).

Response: If I live in the Spirit, I shall also walk by the Spirit (see Galatians 5:25).

Now allow the Spirit to guide you in whatever you need to confess.

Thanksgiving

Listen: "And because you are sons, God has sent forth the Spirit of His Son into your hearts, crying out, 'Abba Father!' Therefore you are no longer a slave but a son, and if a son, then an heir of God through Christ" (Galatians 4:6-7).

Response: "For you did not receive the spirit of bondage again to fear, but you received the Spirit of adoption by whom we cry out, 'Abba, Father'" (Romans 8:15).

Now thank the Lord for the assurance of belonging to Him and being filled with His Spirit.

Silence

Listen: "For we ourselves were also once foolish, disobedient, deceived, serving various lusts and pleasures, living in malice and envy, hateful and hating one another. But when the kindness and the love of God our Savior toward man appeared, not by works of righteousness which we have done, but according to His mercy He saved us, through the washing of regeneration and renewing of the Holy Spirit, whom He poured out on us abundantly through Jesus Christ our Savior, that having been justified by His grace we should become heirs according to the hope of eternal life" (Titus 3:3-7).

Response: "This is a faithful saying, and these things I want you to affirm constantly, that those who have believed in God should be careful to maintain good works. These things are good and profitable to men" (Titus 3:8).

In silence, yield yourself, spirit, soul, mind, and body, to the fresh infilling of the Holy Spirit.

Intercession

Listen: "Likewise the Spirit also helps in our weaknesses. For we do not know what we should pray for as we ought, but the Spirit Himself makes intercession for us with groanings which cannot be uttered. Now He who searches the hearts knows what the mind of the Spirit is, because He makes intercession for the saints according to the will of God" (Romans 8:26-27).

Response: "And we know that all things work together for good to those who love God, to those who are the called according to His purpose" (Romans 8:28).

Now pray for the empowering by the Holy Spirit in the people you know who need strength and courage.

Supplication

Listen: "But as it is written: 'Eye has not seen, nor ear heard, nor have entered into the heart of man the things which God has prepared for those who love Him.' But God has revealed them to us through His Spirit. For the Spirit searches all things, yes, the deep things of God. For what man knows the things of a man except the spirit of the man which is in him? Even so no one knows the things of God except the Spirit of God. Now we have received, not the spirit of the world, but the Spirit who is from God, that we might know the things that have been freely given to us by God.

"These things we also speak, not in words which man's wisdom teaches but which the Holy Spirit teaches, comparing spiritual things with spiritual. But the natural man does not receive the things of the Spirit of God, for they are foolishness to him; nor can he know them, because they are spiritually discerned. But he who is spiritual judges all things, yet he himself is rightly judged by no one" (1 Corinthians 2:9-15).

Response: "For 'who has known the mind of the LORD that he may instruct Him?' But we have the mind of Christ" (1 Corinthians 2:16).

Now pray specifically for the mind of Christ.

Guidance

Listen: "However, when He, the Spirit of truth, has come, He will guide you into all truth; for He will not speak on His own authority, but whatever He hears He will speak; and He will tell you things to come. He will glorify Me, for He will take of what is Mine and declare it to you. All things that the Father has are Mine. Therefore I said that He will take of Mine and declare it to you" (John 16:13).

Response: I pray for the grace of the Lord Jesus, the love of God and the communion of the Holy Spirit (see 2 Corinthians 13:14).

Submit all your concerns to the guidance of the Holy Spirit.

Commitment and Empowering

Listen: "So Jesus said to them again, 'Peace to you! As the Father has sent Me, I also send you.' And when He had said this, He breathed on them and said to them, 'Receive the Holy Spirit'" (John 20:21-22).

"But you shall receive power when the Holy Spirit has come upon you; and you shall be witnesses to Me in Jerusalem, and in all Judea and Samaria, and to the end of the earth" (Acts 1:8).

Response: I accept my calling to "go and tell the people all about this new life" (Acts 5:20 TEV).

Today I am committed to love and serve people so that I may be a witness for my Lord.

Day Seventeen

Preparation

Listen: "Seek the LORD while He may be found, call upon Him while He is near. Let the wicked forsake his way, and the unrighteous man his thoughts; let him return to the LORD, and He will have mercy on him; and to our God, for He will abundantly pardon. 'For my thoughts are not your thoughts, nor are your ways My ways,' says the LORD. 'For as the heavens are higher than the earth, so are My ways higher than your ways, and My thoughts than your thoughts'" (Isaiah 55:6-9).

Response: "For 'who has known the mind of the LORD that he may instruct Him?' But we have the mind of Christ" (1 Corinthians 2:16).

Praise

Listen: "You will keep him in perfect peace, whose mind is stayed on You, because he trusts in You" (Isaiah 26:3).

Response: "Trust in the LORD forever, for in YAH, the LORD, is everlasting strength" (Isaiah 26:4).

Now praise the Lord with freedom and joy.

Confession

Listen: "I have blotted out, like a thick cloud, your transgression, and like a cloud, your sins. Return to Me, for I have redeemed you" (Isaiah 44:22).

Response: "O Lord God, forgive, I pray!" (Amos 7:2).

Now allow the Lord to guide you in your confession. Ask Him to reveal to you anything that stands between you and Him. Then forgive others as He has forgiven you.

Thanksgiving

Listen: "Paul, an apostle of Jesus Christ by the will of God, to the saints who are in Ephesus, and faithful in Christ Jesus: Grace to you and peace from God our Father and the Lord Jesus Christ.

"Blessed be the God and Father of our Lord Jesus Christ, who has blessed us with every spiritual blessing in the heavenly places in Christ, just as He chose us in Him before the foundation of the world, that we should be holy and without blame before Him in love, having predestined us to adoption as sons by Jesus Christ to Himself, according to the good pleasure of His will, to the praise of the glory of His grace, by which He has made us accepted in the Beloved" (Ephesians 1:1-6).

Response: "In Him you also trusted, after you heard the word of truth, the gospel of your salvation; in whom also, having believed, you were sealed with the Holy Spirit of promise, who is the guarantee of our inheritance until the redemption of the purchased possession, to the praise of His glory" (Ephesians 1:13-14).

Now, in the presence of the Lord, think of His lovingkindness to you and give thanks.

Silence

Listen: "I said, 'I will guard my ways, lest I sin with my tongue; I will restrain my mouth with a muzzle, while the wicked are before me.' I was mute with silence, I held my peace even from good; and my sorrow was stirred up. My heart was hot within me; while I was musing the fire burned. Then I spoke with my tongue: 'LORD, make me to know my end, and what is the measure of my days, that I may know how frail I am. Indeed, You have made my days as handbreadths, and my age is as nothing before You; certainly every man at his best state is but vapor. Surely every man walks about like a shadow; surely they busy themselves in vain; he heaps up riches, and does not know who will gather them'" (Psalm 39:1-6).

Response: "And now, Lord, what do I wait for? My hope is in You" (Psalm 39:7).

In the silence, allow the Lord to picture what you are to ask for others and yourself.

Intercession

Listen: "And He bore the sin of many, and made intercession for the transgressors" (Isaiah 53:12).

Response: "For such a High Priest was fitting for us, who is holy, harmless, undefiled, separate from sinners, and has become higher than the heavens" (Hebrews 7:26).

Now pray for your family, friends, enemies, those you need to learn to love, your church, your pastor, church leaders, and the president, governor, and leaders of your city.

Supplication

Listen: "Blessed is the man whose strength is in You, whose heart is set on pilgrimage....They go from strength to strength" (Psalm 84:5,7).

Response: "O LORD God of hosts, hear my prayer; give ear, O God of Jacob!" (Psalm 84:8).

Now list out your needs and thank the Lord in advance for His answers in His timing.

Guidance

Listen: "Who has measured the waters in the hollow of his hand, measured heaven with a span and calculated the dust of the earth in a measure? Weighed the mountains in scales and the hills in a balance? Who has directed the Spirit of the LORD, or as His counselor has taught Him? With whom did He take counsel, and who instructed Him, and taught Him in the path of justice? Who taught Him knowledge, and showed Him the way of understanding?" (Isaiah 40:12-14).

Response: I will not try to direct the Spirit, but be guided by Him.

Now spread out all the decisions you must make and ask the Lord to guide you.

Commitment and Empowering

Listen: "Now may our Lord Jesus Christ Himself, and our God and Father, who has loved us and given us everlasting consolation and good hope by grace, comfort your hearts and establish you in every good word and work" (2 Thessalonians 2:16-17).

Response: May the grace of my Lord Jesus Christ be with me. Amen (see 2 Thessalonians 3:18).

I commit this day to claim the amazing grace of my Lord.

Day Eighteen

Preparation

Listen: "For thus says the Lord God: 'Indeed I Myself will search for My sheep and seek them out. As a shepherd seeks out his flock on the day he is among his scattered sheep, so will I seek out My sheep and deliver them from all the places where they were scattered on a cloudy and dark day....You are My flock, the flock of My pasture; you are men, and I am your God,' says the Lord God" (Ezekiel 34:11-12,31).

Response: "As for you, my son Solomon, know the God of your father, and serve Him with a loyal heart and with a willing mind; for the Lord searches all hearts and understands all the intent of the thoughts. If you seek Him, He will be found by you; but if you forsake Him, He will cast you off forever" (1 Chronicles 28:9).

Praise

Listen: I have come that you may have life, and that you may have it more abundantly (see John 10:10).

Response: "And the grace of our Lord was exceedingly abundant, with faith and love which are in Christ Jesus" (1 Timothy 1:14).

Now praise the Lord, your shepherd, for the gift of an abundant life. Reflect on what Christ means to you and give praise.

Confession

Listen: "I am the good shepherd. The good shepherd gives His life for the sheep. But a hireling, he who is not the shepherd, one who does not own the sheep, sees the wolf coming and leaves the sheep and flees; and the wolf catches the sheep and scatters them. The hireling flees because he is a hireling and does not care about the sheep. I am the good shepherd; and I know My sheep, and am known by My own" (John 10:11-14).

Response: "I have gone astray like a lost sheep; seek Your servant, for I do not forget Your commandments" (Psalm 119:176).

Allow the Lord to bring to your mind those times you have strayed from Him, your shepherd, and then confess them to Him.

Thanksgiving

Listen: "The Lord is my shepherd; I shall not want. He makes me to lie down in green pastures; He leads me beside the still waters. He restores my soul; He leads me in the paths of righteousness for His name's sake. Yea, though I walk through the valley of the shadow of death, I will fear no evil; for You are with me; Your rod and Your staff, they comfort me. You prepare a table before me in the presence of my enemies; you anoint my head with oil; my cup runs over. Surely goodness and mercy shall follow me all the days of my life; and I will dwell in the house of the Lord forever" (Psalm 23).

Now thank the Lord for the ways He has been your shepherd.

Silence

Listen: "Now may the God of peace who brought up our Lord Jesus from the dead, that great Shepherd of the sheep, through the blood of the everlasting covenant, make you complete in every good work to do His will, working in you what is well pleasing in His sight, through Jesus Christ, to whom be glory forever and ever. Amen" (Hebrews 13:20-21).

Response: Shepherd me with your staff (see Micah 7:14).

Now ask the Good Shepherd to lead you.

Intercession

Listen: "And again He entered Capernaum after some days, and it was heard that He was in the house. Immediately many gathered together, so that there was no longer room to receive them, not even near the door. And He preached the word to them. Then they came to Him, bringing a paralytic who was carried by four men. So when they could not come near Him because of the crowd, they uncovered the roof where He was. And when they had broken through, they let down the bed on which the paralytic was lying. When Jesus saw their faith, He said to the paralytic, 'Son, your sins are forgiven you'" (Mark 2:1-5).

Response: *Picture the face of someone you want to bring before Christ as these four men did. Note Christ's affirmation of the faith of the stretcher bearers!*

Supplication

Listen: "Come and hear, all you who fear God, and I will declare what He has done for my soul. I cried to Him with my mouth, and He was extolled with my tongue.

If I regard iniquity in my heart, the Lord will not hear. But certainly God has heard me; He has attended to the voice of my prayer. Blessed be God, who has not turned away my prayer, nor His mercy from me!" (Psalm 66:16-20).

Response: I will trust in the Lord with all my heart, and lean not on my own understanding; in all my ways I will acknowledge Him, and He shall direct my paths (see Proverbs 3:5-6).

Guidance

Listen: "Then Jesus said to them again, 'Most assuredly, I say to you, I am the door of the sheep. All who ever came before Me are thieves and robbers, but the sheep did not hear them. I am the door. If anyone enters by Me, he will be saved, and will go in and out and find pasture'" (John 10:7-9).

Response: "Lead me and guide me" (Psalm 31:3).

Commitment and Empowering

Listen: "Behold, the Lord GOD shall come with a strong hand, and His arm shall rule for Him; behold, His reward is with Him, and His work before Him. He will feed His flock like a shepherd" (Isaiah 40:10).

Response: "The Lamb who is in the midst of the throne will shepherd them and lead them to living fountains of waters" (Revelation 7:17).

Today I will live in the confidence that the Good Shepherd will lead me. I am committed to follow Him.

Day Nineteen

Preparation

Listen: "When You said, 'Seek my face,' my heart said to You, 'Your face, LORD, I will seek'" (Psalm 27:8).

Praise

Listen: "The four living creatures, each having six wings, were full of eyes around and within. And they do not rest day or night, saying: 'Holy, holy, holy, Lord God Almighty, who was and is and is to come!' Whenever the living creatures give glory and honor and thanks to Him who sits on the throne, who lives forever and ever, the twenty-four elders fall down before Him who sits on the throne and worship Him who lives forever and ever, and cast their crowns before the throne, saying: 'You are worthy, O Lord, to receive glory and honor and power; for You created all things, and by Your will they exist and were created'" (Revelation 4:8-11).

Response: "Your way, O God, is in the sanctuary; who is so great a God as our God?" (Psalm 77:13).

Now praise the Lord for Himself in your own words of adoration.

Confession

Listen: "Hear me, O LORD, for Your lovingkindness is good; turn to me according to the multitude of Your tender mercies. And do not hide Your face from Your servant, for I am in trouble; hear me speedily" (Psalm 69:16-17).

Response: "Draw near to my soul, and redeem it" (Psalm 69:18).

Now confess whatever the Lord has shown you that needs His forgiveness.

Thanksgiving

Listen: "Now the Lord is the Spirit; and where the Spirit of the Lord is, there is liberty. But we all, with unveiled face, beholding as in a mirror the glory of the Lord, are being transformed into the same image from glory to glory, just as by the Spirit of the Lord" (2 Corinthians 3:17-18).

Response: "For it is the God who commanded light to shine out of darkness, who has shone in our hearts to give the light of the knowledge of the glory of God in the face of Jesus Christ. But we have this treasure in earthen vessels, that the excellence of the power may be of God and not of us" (2 Corinthians 4:6-7).

Now list out in your mind the blessings of God for which you are thankful today, and thank Him with a grateful heart.

Silence

Listen: "You are the salt of the earth; but if the salt loses its flavor, how shall it be seasoned? It is then good for nothing but to be thrown out and trampled underfoot by men. You are the light of the world. A city that is set on a hill cannot be hidden. Nor do they light a lamp and put it under a basket, but on a lampstand, and it gives light to all who are in the house" (Matthew 5:13-15).

Response: I will let my light shine before others so that they may see what good works You have done in and through me and glorify my Father in heaven (see Matthew 5:16).

Now be silent and listen as you meditate. Ask the Lord to guide your reflection on the needs of others, and what He has to say about what He wants you to be or do.

Intercession

Listen: "Then Moses said to the LORD, 'See, You say to me, "Bring up this people." But You have not let me know whom You will send with me. Yet You have said, "I know you by name, and you have also found grace in My sight." Now therefore I pray, if I have found grace in Your sight, show me now Your way, that I may know You and that I may find grace in Your sight. And consider that this nation is Your people.'

"And He said, 'My Presence will go with you, and I will give you rest.'

"Then he said to Him, 'If Your Presence does not go with us, do not bring us up from here'" (Exodus 33:12-15).

Now intercede for family, friends, people in special need, and the sick.

Supplication

Listen: "Hear my prayer, O LORD, give ear to my supplications! In Your faithfulness answer me, and in Your righteousness. Do not enter into judgment with Your servant, for in Your sight no one living is righteous" (Psalm 143:1-2).

Response: He made Him who knew no sin to be sin for me, that I may become the righteousness of God (see 2 Corinthians 5:21).

Guidance

Listen: "Your ears shall hear a word behind you saying, 'This is the way, walk in it'" (Isaiah 30:21).

Response: "Direct my steps by Your word, and let no iniquity have dominion over me. Redeem me from the oppression of man, that I may keep Your precepts" (Psalm 119:133-134).

Now pray for specific responsibilities and relationships in which you need guidance.

Commitment and Empowering

Listen: "The LORD bless you and keep you; the LORD make His face shine upon you, and be gracious to you; the LORD lift up His countenance upon you, and give you peace" (Numbers 6:24-26).

Response: And whatever I do in word or deed, I will do all in the name of the Lord Jesus, giving thanks to God the Father through Him (see Colossians 3:17).

I will bear in mind no hurting past
To haunt my thoughts today:
I will press on, my mind held fast
To what grace will display.

Day Twenty

Preparation

Listen: "At the noise of the tumult the people shall flee; when You lift Yourself up, the nations shall be scattered" (Isaiah 33:3).

Response: "But as for me, my prayer is to You, O LORD, in the acceptable time; O God, in the multitude of Your mercy, hear me in the truth of Your salvation" (Psalm 69:13).

Praise

Listen: "Wisdom and knowledge will be the stability of your times, and the strength of salvation; the fear of the LORD is His treasure" (Isaiah 33:6).

Response: "Praise the LORD of hosts, for the LORD is good, for His mercy endures forever" (Jeremiah 33:11).

Now praise the Lord in your own words of adoration.

Confession

Listen: "I will cleanse them from all their iniquity by which they have sinned against Me, and I will pardon all their iniquities by which they have sinned and by which they have transgressed against Me" (Jeremiah 33:8).

Response: "I said 'LORD, be merciful to me; heal my soul, for I have sinned against You'" (Psalm 41:4).

Allow the Lord to bring to your mind those things that need His forgiveness.

Thanksgiving

Listen: "Therefore, if anyone is in Christ, he is a new creation; old things have passed away; behold, all things have become new. Now all things are of God, who has reconciled us to Himself through Jesus Christ, and has given us the ministry of reconciliation, that is, that God was in Christ reconciling the world to Himself, not imputing their trespasses to them, and has committed to us the word of reconciliation" (2 Corinthians 5:17-19).

Response: "Blessed be the God and Father of our Lord Jesus Christ, who has blessed us with every spiritual blessing in the heavenly places in Christ" (Ephesians 1:3).

Now take the time to thank the Lord for His grace.

Silence

Listen: "'Therefore be merciful, just as your Father also is merciful. Judge not, and you shall not be judged. Condemn not, and you shall not be condemned. Forgive, and you will be forgiven. Give, and it will be given to you: good measure, pressed down, shaken together, and running over will be put into your bosom. For with the same measure that you use, it will be measured back to you.' And He spoke a parable to them: 'Can the blind lead the blind? Will they not both fall into the ditch?'" (Luke 6:36-39).

Response: Therefore, in Christ, I am a new creation; old things have passed away; behold, all things are new (see 2 Corinthians 5:17).

In silence, allow the Lord to speak His personal word to you.

Intercession

Listen: "I thank God, whom I serve with a pure conscience, as my forefathers did, as without ceasing I remember you in my prayers night and day" (2 Timothy 1:3).

Response: "Being confident of this very thing, that He who has begun a good work in you will complete it until the day of Jesus Christ" (Philippians 1:6).

Now pray for the spiritual growth of loved ones and friends.

Supplication

Listen: "Ho! Everyone who thirsts, come to the waters; and you who have no money, come, buy and eat. Yes, come, buy wine and milk without money and without price. Why do you spend money for what is not bread, and your wages for what does not satisfy? Listen carefully to Me, and eat what is good, and let your soul delight itself in abundance. Incline your ear, and come to Me. Hear, and your soul shall live; and I will make an everlasting covenant with you" (Isaiah 55:1-3).

Response: "Seek the LORD while He may be found, call upon Him while He is near. Let the wicked forsake his way, and the unrighteous man his thoughts; let him return to the LORD, and He will have mercy on him; and to our God, for He will abundantly pardon" (Isaiah 55:6-7).

Now surrender your needs to the Lord's love and care.

Guidance

Consider: Ananias is an unsung hero. Actually, he is an excellent example of one who surrendered his fear and prejudice to follow the guidance from the Lord.

Listen: "But the Lord said to him, 'Go, for he is a chosen vessel of Mine to bear My name before Gentiles, kings, and the children of Israel. For I will show him how many things he must suffer for My name's sake.' And Ananias went his way and entered the house; and laying his hands on him, he said, 'Brother Saul, the Lord Jesus, who appeared to you on the road as you came, has sent me that you may receive your sight and be filled with the Holy Spirit.' Immediately there fell from his eyes something like scales and he received his sight at once; and he arose and was baptized" (Acts 9:15-18).

Response: Guide me, Lord, and help me obey!

Commitment and Empowering

Listen: "The Spirit of the LORD is upon Me, because He has anointed Me to preach the gospel to the poor; He has sent Me to heal the brokenhearted, to proclaim liberty to the captives and recovery of sight to the blind, to set at liberty those who are oppressed, to preach the acceptable year of the LORD" (Luke 4:18-19).

Response: "Now then, we are ambassadors for Christ, as though God were pleading through us: we implore you on Christ's behalf, be reconciled to God" (2 Corinthians 5:20).

Day Twenty-one

Preparation

Listen: "Listen to Me, you who follow after righteousness, you who seek the LORD....I, even I, am He who comforts you....I have put My words in your mouth, I have covered you with the shadow of My hand" (Isaiah 51:1,12,16).

Response: "Hear my prayer, O God; give ear to the words of my mouth" (Psalm 54:2).

Praise

Listen: "I will extol You, my God, O King; and I will bless Your name forever and ever. Every day I will bless You, and I will praise Your name forever and ever. Great is the LORD, and greatly to be praised; and His greatness is unsearchable. One generation shall praise Your works to another, and shall declare Your mighty acts" (Psalm 145:1-4).

Response: "I will meditate on the glorious splendor of Your majesty, and on Your wondrous works. Men shall speak of the might of Your awesome acts, and I will declare Your greatness. They shall utter the memory of Your great goodness, and shall sing of Your righteousness" (Psalm 145:5-7).

Think magnificently of God—His attributes, His nature, and His glory—and then praise Him with your whole heart.

Confession

Listen: "The LORD is gracious and full of compassion, slow to anger and great in mercy. The LORD is good to all, and His tender mercies are over all His works" (Psalm 145:8-9).

Response: "The LORD is righteous in all His ways, gracious in all His works. The LORD is near to all who call upon Him, to all who call upon Him in truth. He will fulfill the desire of those who fear Him; He also will hear their cry and save them" (Psalm 145:17-18).

Claim the forgiveness for what you have done or said that needs His forgiveness.

Thanksgiving

Listen: "Most assuredly, I say to you, he who hears My word and believes in Him who sent Me has everlasting life, and shall not come into judgment, but has passed from death into life" (John 5:24).

Response: And this is eternal life, that I may know You, the only true God, and Jesus Christ whom You have sent (see John 17:3).

Thanksgiving is the memory of the heart. Remember what the Lord has done for you and express your gratitude.

Silence

Listen: "And I, if I am lifted up from the earth, will draw all peoples to Myself" (John 12:32).

Response: "I have been crucified with Christ; it is no longer I who live, but Christ lives in me; and the life which I now live in the flesh I live by faith in the Son of God, who loved me and gave Himself for me" (Galatians 2:20).

Picture your life completely under the control of the Lord. Seeking first His kingdom, what needs to be changed, renewed, released?

Intercession

Listen: "Hezekiah received the letter from the hand of the messengers, and read it; and Hezekiah went up to the house of the LORD, and spread it before the LORD" (2 Kings 19:14).

Now spread out before the Lord the needs of people on your heart and claim the Lord's blessing, will, and power for them.

Supplication

Listen: "Casting all your care upon Him" (1 Peter 5:7).

Response: He cares for me (see 1 Peter 5:7).

Open your heart to the Lord and trust Him with whatever causes you worry or anxiety today.

Guidance

Listen: "For You are my rock and my fortress; therefore, for Your name's sake, lead me and guide me" (Psalm 31:3).

Now ask the Lord for the steps He wants you to take today.

Commitment and Empowering

Listen: "Who knows whether you have come to the kingdom for such a time as this?" (Esther 4:14).

Response: And whatever I do in word or deed, I will do in the name of the Lord Jesus, giving thanks to God the Father through Him (see Colossians 3:17).

The Lord gives the day; He will show the way.

Day Twenty-two

Preparation

Listen: "But the hour is coming, and now is, when the true worshipers will worship the Father in spirit and truth; for the Father is seeking such to worship Him. God is Spirit, and those who worship Him must worship in spirit and truth" (John 4:23-24).

Response: "You are worthy, O Lord, to receive glory and honor and power; for You created all things, and by Your will they exist and were created" (Revelation 4:11).

Praise

Listen: "I will love You, O LORD, my strength. The LORD is my rock and my fortress and my deliverer; my God, my strength, in whom I will trust; my shield and the horn of my salvation, my stronghold" (Psalm 18:1-2).

Response: "I will call upon the LORD, who is worthy to be praised; so shall I be saved from my enemies" (Psalm 18:3).

Now in your own words, tell the Lord how much you love Him. Adore and exalt Him with your whole heart.

Confession

Listen: "You shall no more worship the work of your hands" (Micah 5:13).

Response: He has shown me what is good; and what does the Lord require of me but to do justly, to love mercy, and to walk humbly with my God (see Micah 6:8).

Allow the Lord to bring to your mind what needs to be confessed and forgiven.

Thanksgiving

Listen: "Give to the LORD the glory due His name; bring an offering, and come before Him. Oh, worship the Lord in the beauty of holiness!" (1 Chronicles 16:29).

Response: "Oh, give thanks to the Lord, for He is good! For His mercy endures forever. And say, 'Save us, O God of our salvation; gather us together, and deliver us from the Gentiles, to give thanks to Your holy name, to triumph in Your praise'" (1 Chronicles 16:34-35).

Now thank the Lord for His mercy and constant care.

Silence

Listen: "Thus He showed me: Behold, the Lord stood on a wall made with a plumb line, with a plumb line in His hand" (Amos 7:7).

Response: Lord, lower Your plumb line on my life. Show me what is in or out of plumb.

Intercession

Listen: "I sought for a man among them who would... stand in the gap before Me on behalf of the land...but I found no one" (Ezekiel 22:30).

"He saw that there was no man, and wondered that there was no intercessor" (Isaiah 59:16).

Response: "I am ready" (2 Corinthians 12:14).

Now pray for the needs of people—family, friends, fellow workers, the sick, troubled, and those facing great challenges.

Supplication

Listen: "I am with you....I will strengthen you, yes, I will help you" (Isaiah 41:10).

Response: "The LORD is my strength and song" (Exodus 15:2).

Trust the Lord with the needs of your own life.

Guidance

Listen: "If you extend your soul to the hungry and satisfy the afflicted soul, then your light shall dawn in the darkness, and your darkness shall be as the noonday" (Isaiah 58:10).

Response: "The LORD will guide you continually, and satisfy your soul in drought, and strengthen your bones; you shall be like a watered garden, and like a spring of water, whose waters do not fail" (Isaiah 58:11).

Claim the Lord's guidance for decisions and directions.

Commitment and Empowering

Listen: "But you are not in the flesh but in the Spirit, if indeed the Spirit of God dwells in you. Now if anyone does not have the Spirit of Christ, he is not His. And if Christ is in you, the body is dead because of sin, but the Spirit is life because of righteousness. But if the Spirit of Him who raised Jesus from the dead dwells in you, He who raised Christ from the dead will also give life to your mortal bodies through His Spirit who dwells in you" (Romans 8:9-11).

Response: "For as many as are led by the Spirit of God, these are sons of God" (Romans 8:14).

With this assurance, I will have a great day!

Day Twenty-three

Preparation

Listen: "Yet I will not forget you. See, I have inscribed you on the palms of My hands" (Isaiah 49:15b-16a).

Response: "For You are my rock and my fortress; therefore, for Your name's sake, lead me and guide me.... Into Your hand I commit my spirit; You have redeemed me, O LORD God of truth....But as for me, I trust in You, O LORD; I say, 'You are my God.' My times are in Your hand" (Psalm 31:3,5,14-15a).

Praise

Listen: "Oh, how great is Your goodness, which You have laid up for those who fear You, which You have prepared for those who trust in You in the presence of the sons of men!" (Psalm 31:19).

Response: "Oh, love the LORD, all you His saints! For the Lord preserves the faithful, and fully repays the proud person. Be of good courage, and He shall strengthen your heart, all you who hope in the LORD" (Psalm 31:23-24).

Express your love for the Lord in your own words of praise and adoration.

Confession

Listen: "O LORD, You have searched me and known me. You know my sitting down and my rising up; You understand my thought afar off. You comprehend my path and my lying down, and are acquainted with all my ways. For there is not a word on my tongue, but behold, O LORD, You know it altogether. You have hedged me behind and before, and laid Your hand upon me. Such knowledge is too wonderful for me; it is high, I cannot attain it" (Psalm 139:1-6).

Response: "Where can I go from Your Spirit? Or where can I flee from Your presence? If I ascend into heaven, You are there; if I make my bed in hell, behold, You are there. If I take the wings of the morning, and dwell in the uttermost parts of the sea, even there Your hand shall lead me, and Your right hand shall hold me. If I say, 'Surely the darkness shall fall on me,' even the night shall be light about me; indeed the darkness shall not hide from You, but the night shines as the day; the darkness and the light are both alike to You....

"Search me, O God, and know my heart; try me, and know my anxieties; and see if there is any wicked way in me, and lead me in the way everlasting" (Psalm 139:7-12,23-24).

Allow the Lord to search your heart, and then make your confession and receive forgiveness.

Thanksgiving

Listen: "Behold what manner of love the Father has bestowed on us, that we should be called children of God! Therefore the world does not know us, because it did not know Him. Beloved, now we are children of God; and it has not yet been revealed what we shall be, but we know that when He is revealed, we shall be like Him, for we shall see Him as He is. And everyone who has this hope in Him purifies himself, just as He is pure" (1 John 3:1-3).

Response: *Pause now to thank the Lord for all He has done for you.*

Silence

Listen: "I remember the days of old; I meditate on all Your works; I muse on the work of Your hands" (Psalm 143:5).

Response: "But now, O LORD, You are our Father; we are the clay, and You our potter; and all we are the work of Your hand" (Isaiah 64:8).

In the silence, yield the clay of your life to the Potter. "Have Your own way, Lord. You are the Potter, I am the clay."

Intercession

Listen: "The LORD upholds all who fall, and raises up all those who are bowed down" (Psalm 145:14).

Response: "The LORD is righteous in all His ways, gracious in all His works. The LORD is near to all who call upon Him, to all who call upon Him in truth. He will fulfill the desire of those who fear Him; He also will hear their cry and save them" (Psalm 145:17-19).

Now intercede for those in authority—the president, vice president, the governor of your state, city officials, and those who carry heavy responsibilities in leadership.

Supplication

Listen: "Also your people shall all be righteous; they shall inherit the land forever, the branch of My planting, the work of My hands, that I may be glorified" (Isaiah 60:21).

Response: Hear my prayer, O Lord!

Guidance

Listen: "Nevertheless I am continually with You; You hold me by my right hand. You will guide me with Your counsel, and afterward receive me to glory" (Psalm 73:23-24).

Response: "Whom have I in heaven but You? And there is none upon earth that I desire besides You. My flesh and my heart fail; but God is the strength of my heart and my portion forever....But it is good for me to draw near to God; I have put my trust in the Lord GOD, that I may declare all Your works" (Psalm 73:25-26,28).

Now pray specifically for upcoming opportunities and challenges.

Commitment and Empowering

Listen: "Commit your works to the LORD, and your thoughts will be established" (Proverbs 16:3).

Response: I commit my way to the Lord, and trust also in Him, and He shall bring it to pass....I rest in the Lord and wait patiently for Him (Psalm 37:5,7).

Day Twenty-four

Preparation

Listen: "Lift up your heads, O you gates! And be lifted up, you everlasting doors! And the King of glory shall come in. Who is this King of glory? The LORD strong and mighty, the LORD mighty in battle. Lift up your heads, O you gates! Lift up, you everlasting doors! And the King of glory shall come in. Who is this King of glory? The LORD of hosts, He is the King of glory. Selah" (Psalm 24:7-10).

Response: "Teach me Your way, O LORD; I will walk in Your truth; unite my heart to fear Your name. I will praise You, O Lord my God, with all my heart, and I will glorify Your name forevermore" (Psalm 86:11).

Praise

Listen: "And one cried to another and said, 'Holy, holy, holy is the Lord of hosts; the whole earth is full of His glory!'" (Isaiah 6:3).

Response: "The four living creatures, each having six wings, were full of eyes around and within. And they do not rest day or night, saying: 'Holy, holy, holy, Lord God Almighty, who was and is and is to come!'" (Revelation 4:8).

Now praise the Lord in your own words with adoration and love.

Confession

Listen: "To the Lord our God belong mercy and forgiveness, though we have rebelled against Him" (Daniel 9:9).

Response: "O Lord, hear! O Lord, forgive! O Lord, listen and act! Do not delay for Your own sake, my God, for Your city and Your people are called by Your name" (Daniel 9:19).

Now claim that through the cross you have been forgiven. Accept the forgiveness that is already yours. Allow the Lord to hear your confession and listen for His assurance of forgiveness and His power to free you from repetitive patterns of sin and failure.

Thanksgiving

Listen: "For God so loved the world that He gave His only begotten Son, that whoever believes in Him should not perish but have everlasting life. For God did not send His Son into the world to condemn the world, but that the world through Him might be saved" (John 3:16-17).

Response: "Therefore, having been justified by faith, we have peace with God through our Lord Jesus Christ, through whom also we have access by faith into this grace in which we stand, and rejoice in the hope of the glory of God" (Romans 5:1-2).

Now express in your own words your gratitude for the gift of abundant and eternal life in Christ.

Silence

Listen: "Blessed are the poor in spirit, for theirs is the kingdom of heaven. Blessed are those who mourn, for they shall be comforted. Blessed are the meek, for they shall inherit the earth. Blessed are those who hunger and thirst for righteousness, for they shall be filled. Blessed are the merciful, for they shall obtain mercy. Blessed are the pure in heart, for they shall see God. Blessed are the peacemakers, for they shall be called sons of God. Blessed are those who are persecuted for righteousness' sake, for theirs is the kingdom of heaven" (Matthew 5:3-10).

Response: Lord, in this silence, show me which of these blessed attitudes I need most today.

Intercession

Listen: "Beloved, I pray that you may prosper in all things and be in health, just as your soul prospers" (3 John 2).

Response: "And my God shall supply all your needs according to His riches in glory by Christ Jesus" (Philippians 4:19).

Now claim that promise for the people on your prayer list.

Supplication

Listen: "I will not leave you nor forsake you. Be strong and of good courage" (Joshua 1:5,6).

Response: "Save me, O God, by Your name, and vindicate me by Your strength. Hear my prayer, O God; give ear to the words of my mouth" (Psalm 54:1-2).

Now give over to the Lord's control the problems and difficulties that confront you today.

Guidance

Listen: "Teach me to do Your will, for You are my God; Your Spirit is good. Lead me in the land of uprightness" (Psalm 143:10).

Response: "Revive me, O LORD, for Your name's sake! For Your righteousness' sake bring my soul out of trouble" (Psalm 143:11).

Now list out the decisions and choices you must make and thank the Lord in advance for His guidance.

Commitment and Empowering

Listen: "But all things that are exposed are made manifest by the light, for whatever makes manifest is light. Therefore He says: 'Awake, you who sleep, arise from the dead, and Christ will give you light.' See then that you walk circumspectly, not as fools but as wise, redeeming the time, because the days are evil. Therefore do not be unwise, but understand what the will of the Lord is" (Ephesians 5:13-17).

Response: I will keep on being filled with the Spirit (see Ephesians 5:18).

Now commit yourself anew to the Lord; He is committed to helping you. Because of His greatness, this is going to be a great day!

Day Twenty-five

Preparation

Listen: "You are My friends if you do whatever I command you. No longer do I call you servants, for a servant does not know what his master is doing; but I have called you friends, for all things that I heard from My Father I have made known to you. You did not choose Me, but I chose you and appointed you that you should go and bear fruit, and that your fruit should remain, that whatever you ask the Father in My name He may give you" (John 15:14-16).

Response: "I press toward the goal for the prize of the upward call of God in Christ Jesus" (Philippians 3:14).

Praise

Listen: "But you are a chosen generation, a royal priesthood, a holy nation, His own special people, that you may proclaim the praises of Him who called you out of darkness into His marvelous light; who once were not a people but are now the people of God, who had not obtained mercy but now have obtained mercy" (1 Peter 2:9-10).

Response: Praise the Lord!

Confession

Listen: "For when we were still without strength, in due time Christ died for the ungodly. For scarcely for a righteous man will one die; yet perhaps for a good man someone would even dare to die. But God demonstrates His own love toward us, in that while we were still sinners, Christ died for us" (Romans 5:6-8).

Response: I claim my forgiveness through the cross.

Thanksgiving

Listen: "Much more then, having now been justified by His blood, we shall be saved from wrath through Him. For if when we were enemies we were reconciled to God through the death of His Son, much more, having been reconciled, we shall be saved by His life" (Romans 5:9-10).

Response: And not only that, but I also rejoice in God through Jesus Christ, through whom I have now received the reconciliation (see Romans 5:11).

Silence

Listen: "Woe to him who strives with his Maker! Let the potsherd strive with the potsherds of the earth. Shall the clay say to him who forms it, 'What are you making?' Or shall your handiwork say, 'He has no hands'?" (Isaiah 45:9).

Response: For I am His workmanship, created in Christ Jesus for good works, which God prepared beforehand that I should walk in them (see Ephesians 2:10).

Intercession

Consider: Peter was praying on a housetop in Joppa. The Lord put Cornelius on his heart. At the same time Cornelius was praying for God's truth. Read Acts 10. It reveals how the Lord sometimes interrupts our prayers to let us in on His agenda.

Response: Lord, help me put Your will on the top of my agenda. Make me responsive to Your new directions for my life.

Supplication

Listen: "But Jesus said, 'Somebody touched Me, for I perceived power going out from Me.' Now when the woman saw that she was not hidden, she came trembling; and falling down before Him, she declared to Him in the presence of all the people the reason she had touched Him and how she was healed immediately. And He said to her, 'Daughter, be of good cheer; your faith has made you well. Go in peace'" (Luke 8:46-48).

Response: Lord, my prayer is reaching out to You with a touch of faith. Here are my needs. May I hear you say, "Be of good cheer; your faith has made you well. Go in peace."

Guidance

Listen: "With eyes wide open to the mercies of God, I beg you...as an act of intelligent worship, to give your bodies, as a living sacrifice, consecrated to Him and acceptable to Him. Don't let the world around you squeeze you into its own mold, but let God remold your minds from within, so that you may prove in practice that the plan of God for you is good, meets all His demands, and moves toward the goal of true maturity" (Romans 12:1-2 PHILLIPS).

Response: Lord, guide me so I can realize my full maturity in the fullness of Christ.

Commitment and Empowering

Listen: What do you have to bring to people and a needy world? Consider Paul's assurance: "But I know that when I come to you, I shall come in the fullness of the blessing of the gospel of Christ" (Romans 15:29).

Response: I claim Christ's promise, "I am with you always" (Matthew 28:20).

Day Twenty-six

Preparation

Listen: "Call upon Me in the day of trouble; I will deliver you, and you shall glorify Me" (Psalm 50:15).

Response: "But the salvation of the righteous is from the LORD; He is their strength in the time of trouble" (Psalm 37:39).

Praise

Listen: "For You are great, and do wondrous things; You alone are God" (Psalm 86:10).

Response: "Teach me Your way, O LORD; I will walk in Your truth; unite my heart to fear Your name. I will praise You, O LORD my God, with all my heart, and I will glorify Your name forevermore" (Psalm 86:11-12).

Now praise the Lord in your own words.

Confession

In preparation for confession today, read Luke 10:38-42.

Listen: "You are worried and troubled about many things. But one thing is needed, and Mary has chosen that good part" (Luke 10:41-42).

Response: I will seek first the kingdom of God....I will not worry about tomorrow, for tomorrow will worry about its own things. Sufficient for the day is its own trouble (see Matthew 6:33-34).

Now make your confession of the worries of your life that expose a need to trust the Lord more fully.

Thanksgiving

Listen: "I will praise You with my whole heart; before the gods I will sing praises to You. I will worship toward Your holy temple, and praise Your name for Your loving-kindness and Your truth; for You have magnified Your word above all Your name. In the day when I cried out, You answered me, and made me bold with strength in my soul" (Psalm 138:1-3).

Response: "Though I walk in the midst of trouble, You will revive me" (Psalm 138:7a).

Take time to thank the Lord for His help in time of trouble.

Silence

Listen: "Blessed be the God and Father of our Lord Jesus Christ, the Father of mercies and God of all comfort, who comforts us in all our tribulation, that we may be able to comfort those who are in any trouble, with the comfort with which we ourselves are comforted by God" (2 Corinthians 1:3-4).

Response: "I am exceedingly joyful in...tribulation" (2 Corinthians 7:4).

Claim the Lord's presence and power to give you strength and courage.

Intercession

Listen: "Hear my prayer, O LORD, and let my cry come to You. Do not hide Your face from me in the day of my trouble; incline Your ear to me; in the day that I call, answer me speedily" (Psalm 102:1-2).

Response: *Allow the Lord to bring to mind people you know are troubled. Ask how to pray.*

Supplication

Listen: "The LORD will perfect that which concerns me; Your mercy, O LORD, endures forever; do not forsake the works of Your hands" (Psalm 138:8).

Response: Hear my prayer, O Lord.

Guidance

Listen: "Oh, send out Your light and Your truth! Let them lead me" (Psalm 43:3).

Response: "For You are my rock and my fortress; therefore, for Your name's sake, lead me and guide me" (Psalm 31:3).

    Now ask the Lord for specific guidance for your decisions and responsibilities.

Commitment and Empowering

Listen: "And who is he who will harm you if you become followers of what is good? But even if you should suffer for righteousness' sake, you are blessed. 'And do not be afraid of their threats, nor be troubled.' But sanctify the Lord God in your hearts, and always be ready to give a defense to everyone who asks you

a reason for the hope that is in you, with meekness and fear; having a good conscience, that when
they defame you as evildoers, those who revile your
good conduct in Christ may be ashamed"
(1 Peter 3:13-16).

Response: To be continued in Jesus' name!

Day Twenty-seven

Preparation

Listen: "But from there you will seek the LORD your God, and you will find Him if you seek Him with all your heart and with all your soul" (Deuteronomy 4:29).

Response: "The LORD has heard my supplication; the LORD will receive my prayer" (Psalm 6:9).

Praise

Listen: "Jesus answered him, 'The first of all the commandments is: "Hear, O Israel, the LORD our God, the LORD is one. And you shall love the LORD your God with all your heart, with all your soul, with all your mind, and with all your strength." This is the first commandment. And the second, like it, is this: "You shall love your neighbor as yourself." There is no other commandment greater than these'" (Mark 12:29-31).

Response: "I will praise You, O LORD, with my whole heart; I will tell of all Your marvelous works. I will be glad and rejoice in You; I will sing praise to Your name, O Most High" (Psalm 9:1-2).

Now express your love for the Lord.

Confession

Listen: "Seek the LORD while He may be found, call upon Him while He is near. Let the wicked forsake his way, and the unrighteous man his thoughts; let him return to the LORD, and He will have mercy on him; and to our God, for He will abundantly pardon" (Isaiah 55:6-7).

Response: "The LORD is gracious and full of compassion, slow to anger and great in mercy. The LORD is good to all, and His tender mercies are over all His works" (Psalm 145:8-9).

Allow the Lord to show you what needs to be confessed.

Thanksgiving

Listen: "Oh, give thanks to the LORD! Call upon His name; make known His deeds among the peoples" (Psalm 105:1).

Response: "Sing to Him, sing psalms to Him; talk of all His wondrous works! Glory in His holy name; let the hearts of those rejoice who seek the LORD! Seek the LORD and His strength; seek His face evermore! Remember His marvelous works which He has done, His wonders, and the judgments of His mouth" (Psalm 105:2-5).

Now thank the Lord for His love and forgiveness.

Silence

Listen: "Search me, O God, and know my heart; try me, and know my anxieties" (Psalm 139:23).

Response: "Lead me in the way everlasting" (Psalm 139:24).

In the silence, allow the Lord to reveal the deeper causes of anxiety and seek first His priorities in your life.

Intercession

Listen: "So I say to you, ask, and it will be given to you; seek, and you will find; knock, and it will be opened to you. For everyone who asks receives, and he who seeks finds, and to him who knocks it will be opened. If a son asks for bread from any father among you, will he give him a stone? Or if he asks for a fish, will he give him a serpent instead of a fish? Or if he asks for an egg, will he offer him a scorpion? If you then, being evil, know how to give good gifts to your children, how much more will your heavenly Father give the Holy Spirit to those who ask Him!" (Luke 11:9-13).

Response: Lord, show me what You want in the lives of the people for whom I am concerned and free me to ask for what You want to give, do, and provide.

Supplication

Listen: "Then He spoke a parable to them, that men always ought to pray and not lose heart, saying: 'There was in a certain city a judge who did not fear God nor regard man. Now there was a widow in that city; and she came to him, saying, "Get justice for me from my adversary." And he would not for a while; but afterward he said within himself, "Though I do not fear God nor regard man, yet because this widow troubles me I will avenge her, lest by her continual coming she weary me." '

"Then the Lord said, 'Hear what the unjust judge said. And shall God not avenge His own elect who cry out day and night to Him, though He bears long with them? I tell you that He will avenge them speedily. Nevertheless, when the Son of Man comes, will He really find faith on the earth?' " (Luke 18:1-8)

Response: "LORD, I cry out to You; make haste to me! Give ear to my voice when I cry out to You" (Psalm 141:1).

Now open your heart to the Lord. He cares about what concerns you.

Guidance

Listen: "From the end of the earth I will cry to You, when my heart is overwhelmed; lead me to the rock that is higher than I" (Psalm 61:2).

Response: "Let us therefore come boldly to the throne of grace, that we may obtain mercy and find grace in time of need" (Hebrews 4:16).

Claim that with the Lord, the future is a friend. What He guides, He provides.

Commitment and Empowering

Listen: "Whoever believes that Jesus is the Christ is born of God, and everyone who loves Him who begot also loves him who is begotten of Him. By this we know that we love the children of God, when we love God and keep His commandments. For this is the love of God, that we keep His commandments. And His commandments are not burdensome. For whatever is born of God overcomes the world. And this is the victory that has overcome the world—our faith. Who is he who overcomes the world, but he who believes that Jesus is the Son of God?" (1 John 5:1-5).

Response: To be continued in Jesus' name!

Day Twenty-eight

Preparation

Listen: "Fear not, I will help you" (Isaiah 41:13).

Response: "Blessed be the LORD, because He has heard the voice of my supplications! The LORD is my strength and my shield; my heart trusted in Him, and I am helped; therefore my heart greatly rejoices, and with my song I will praise Him" (Psalm 28:6-7).

Praise

Listen: "Our help is in the name of the LORD, who made heaven and earth" (Psalm 124:8).

Response: "The LORD is my strength and my shield; my heart trusted in Him, and I am helped; therefore my heart greatly rejoices, and with my song I will praise Him" (Psalm 28:7).

Express your love for the Lord.

Confession

Listen: "For He made Him who knew no sin to be sin for us, that we might become the righteousness of God in Him" (2 Corinthians 5:21).

Response:　　"For He says, 'In an acceptable time I have heard you, and in the day of salvation I have helped you'" (2 Corinthians 6:2).

　　　　　　　Allow the Lord to lead you in your confession of what needs His forgiveness.

Thanksgiving

Listen:　　"A new commandment I give to you, that you love one another; as I have loved you, that you also love one another. By this all will know that you are My disciples, if you have love for one another" (see John 13:34-35).

Response:　　You are the vine, I am the branch. Apart from You I can do nothing (see John 15:5).

　　　　　　　Thank the Lord for His faithful love.

Silence

Listen:　　"So when they had eaten breakfast, Jesus said to Simon Peter, 'Simon, son of Jonah, do you love Me more than these?' He said to Him, 'Yes, Lord; You know that I love You.' He said to him, 'Feed My lambs.' He said to him again a second time, 'Simon, son of Jonah, do you love Me?' He said to Him, 'Yes, Lord; You know that I love You.' He said to him, 'Tend My sheep.' He said to him the third time, 'Simon, son of Jonah, do you love Me?' Peter was grieved because He said to him the third time, 'Do you love Me?'And he said to Him, 'Lord, You know all things; You know that I love You.' Jesus said to him, 'Feed my sheep'" (John 21:15-17).

Response:　　I love Him because He first loved me (see 1 John 4:19).

Intercession

Listen:　　"You have heard that it was said, 'You shall love your neighbor and hate your enemy.' But I say to you, love your enemies, bless those who curse you, do good to those who hate you, and pray for those who spitefully use you and persecute you, that you may be sons of your Father in heaven; for He makes His sun rise on the evil and on the good, and sends rain on the just and on the unjust. For if you love those who love you, what reward have you? Do not even the tax collectors do the same? And if you greet your brethren only, what do you do more than others? Do not even the tax collectors do so? Therefore you shall be perfect, just as your Father in heaven is perfect" (Matthew 5:43-48).

Response: Hear my prayer for those who have hurt me.

Supplication

Listen: "Oh, give thanks to the LORD! Call upon His name; make known His deeds among the peoples! Sing to Him, sing psalms to Him; talk of all His wondrous works! Glory in His holy name; let the hearts of those rejoice who seek the LORD!" (Psalm 105:1-3).

Response: "Seek the LORD and His strength; seek His face evermore! Remember His marvelous works which He has done, His wonders, and the judgments of His mouth" (Psalm 105:4-5).

Guidance

Consider: Paul was guided in his missionary journey. The Holy Spirit forbade, did not permit, and finally got the apostle to Troas where He could give him the vision to go to Macedonia. The Spirit sometimes says, "No," so He can direct us to His "Yes!"

Listen: "Now when they had gone through Phrygia and the region of Galatia, they were forbidden by the Holy Spirit to preach the word in Asia. After they had come to Mysia, they tried to go into Bithynia, but the Spirit did not permit them. So passing by Mysia, they came down to Troas. And a vision appeared to Paul in the night. A man of Macedonia stood and pleaded with him, saying, 'Come over to Macedonia and help us.' Now after he had seen the vision, immediately we sought to go to Macedonia, concluding that the Lord had called us to preach the gospel to them" (Acts 16:6-10).

Response: Holy Spirit, help me to accept closed doors as preparation for seeing and going through the open door You have set before me.

Commitment and Empowering

Listen: "Till we all come to the unity of the faith and the knowledge of the Son of God, to a perfect man, to the measure of the stature of the fullness of Christ; that we should no longer be children, tossed to and fro and carried about with every wind of doctrine, by the trickery of men, in the cunning craftiness of deceitful plotting, but, speaking the truth in love, may grow up in all things into Him who is the head—Christ—from whom the whole body, joined and knit together by what every joint supplies, according to the effective working by which every part does its share, causes growth of the body for the edifying of itself in love" (Ephesians 4:13-16).

Response: Amen! To be continued in Christ's name!

Day Twenty-nine

Preparation

Listen: "LORD, You have heard the desire of the humble; You will prepare their heart; You will cause Your ear to hear" (Psalm 10:17).

Response: "He has put a new song in my mouth—praise to our God; many will see it and fear, and will trust in the LORD" (Psalm 40:3).

Praise

Listen: "Praise the LORD! Praise, O servants of the LORD, praise the name of the LORD! Blessed be the name of the LORD from this time forth and forevermore! From the rising of the sun to its going down the LORD's name is to be praised" (Psalm 113:1-3).

Response: "The Lord is high above all nations, and His glory above the heavens. Who is like the LORD our God, who dwells on high, who humbles Himself to behold the things that are in the heavens and in the earth?" (Psalm 113:4-6).

Now praise the Lord for Himself in your own words of adoration.

Confession

Listen: In the following parable, Jesus calls us beyond duty to delight, and to confession for doing only our duty.

"And which of you, having a servant plowing or tending sheep, will say to him when he has come in from the field, 'Come at once and sit down to eat'? But will he not rather say to him, 'Prepare something for my supper, and gird yourself and serve me till I have eaten and drunk, and afterward you will eat and drink'? Does he thank that servant because he did the things that were commanded him? I think not. So likewise you, when you have done all those things which you are commanded, say, 'We are unprofitable servants. We have done what was our duty to do'" (Luke 17:7-10).

Response: *Now confess your neglect of great things you could have done because you were satisfied with the minimum standard of duty.*

Thanksgiving

Listen: "Make a joyful shout to the LORD, all you lands! Serve the LORD with gladness; come before His presence with singing. Know that the LORD, He is God; it is He who has made us, and not we ourselves; we are His people and the sheep of His pasture. Enter into His gates with thanksgiving, and into His courts with praise. Be thankful to Him and bless His name. For the LORD is good; His mercy is everlasting, and His truth endures to all generations" (Psalm 100).

Response: "You have put gladness in my heart, more than in the season that their grain and wine increased" (Psalm 4:7).

Now list out in your mind the blessings of God for which you are thankful today, and thank Him with a grateful heart.

Silence

Listen: "Assuredly, I say to you, unless you are converted and become as little children, you will by no means enter the kingdom of heaven. Therefore whoever humbles himself as this little child is the greatest in the kingdom of heaven. Whoever receives one little child like this in My name receives Me" (Matthew 18:3-5).

Response: "God...gives grace to the humble" (1 Peter 5:5).

Intercession

Listen: "Now when Jesus had entered Capernaum, a centurion came to Him, pleading with Him, saying, 'Lord, my servant is lying at home paralyzed, dreadfully tormented.' And Jesus said to him, 'I will come and heal him.' The centurion answered and said, 'Lord, I am not worthy that You should come under my roof. But only speak a word, and my servant will be healed. For I also am a man under authority, having soldiers under me. And I say to this one, "Go," and he goes; and to another, "Come," and he comes; and to my servant, "Do this," and he does it.' When Jesus heard it, He marveled, and said to those who followed, 'Assuredly, I say to you, I have not found such great faith, not even in Israel!' " (Matthew 8:5-10).

Response: The Lord desires intercessors. I will be one of them today and bring the needs of people to Him with confidence like this centurion.

Now intercede for family, friends, people in special need, and the sick.

Supplication

Listen: "Peace I leave with you, My peace I give to you; not as the world gives do I give to you. Let not your heart be troubled, neither let it be afraid" (John 14:27).

Response: I will be anxious for nothing, but in everything by prayer and supplication, with thanksgiving, I will let my requests be made known to God; and the peace of God, which surpasses all understanding, will guard my heart and mind through Christ Jesus (see Philippians 4:6-7).

Guidance

Listen: "However, when He, the Spirit of truth, has come, He will guide you into all truth; for He will not speak on His own authority, but whatever He hears He will speak; and He will tell you things to come" (John 16:13).

Response: I believe in You, Holy Spirit, I receive You by faith, I ask You to guide me.

Commitment and Empowering

Listen: "And to the angel of the church in Philadelphia write, 'These things says He who is holy, He who is true, "He who has the key of David, He who opens and no one shuts, and shuts and no one opens": I know your works. See, I have set before you an open door, and no one can shut it; for you have a little strength, have kept My word, and have not denied My name....

"Because you have kept My command to persevere, I also will keep you from the hour of trial which shall come upon the whole world, to test those who dwell on the earth. Behold, I am coming quickly! Hold fast what you have, that no one may take your crown. He who overcomes, I will make him a pillar in the temple of My God, and he shall go out no more. And I will write on him the name of My God and the name of the city of My God, the New Jerusalem, which comes down out of heaven from My God. And I will write on him My new name. He who has an ear, let him hear what the Spirit says to the churches'" (Revelation 3:7-8,10-13).

Response: To be continued in Jesus' name!

Day Thirty

Preparation

Listen: "Your Father knows the things you have need of before you ask Him" (Matthew 6:8).

Response: "Ask, and it will be given to you; seek, and you will find; knock, and it will be opened to you. For everyone who asks receives, and he who seeks finds, and to him who knocks it will be opened. Or what man is there among you who, if his son asks for bread, will give him a stone? Or if he asks for a fish, will he give him a serpent? If you then, being evil, know how to give good gifts to your children, how much more will your Father who is in heaven give good things to those who ask Him!" (Matthew 7:7-11).

Praise

Listen: "Blessed be the Lord, who daily loads us with benefits, the God of our salvation!" (Psalm 68:19).

Response: "O God, You are more awesome than Your holy places. The God of Israel is He who gives strength and power to His people" (Psalm 68:35).

Now pause to praise the Lord for the joy He gives to your life.

Confession

Listen: "Therefore be merciful, just as your Father also is merciful. Judge not, and you shall not be judged. Condemn not, and you shall not be condemned. Forgive, and you will be forgiven. Give, and it will be given to you: good measure, pressed down, shaken together, and running over will be put into your bosom. For with the same measure that you use, it will be measured back to you" (Luke 6:36-38).

Response: "And the tax collector, standing afar off, would not so much as raise his eyes to heaven, but beat his breast, saying, 'God be merciful to me a sinner!'" (Luke 18:13).

Now confess whatever the Lord brings to mind that needs His cleansing forgiveness.

Thanksgiving

Listen: "Therefore I say to you, do not worry about your life, what you will eat or what you will drink; nor about your body, what you will put on. Is not life more than food and the body more than clothing? Look at the birds of the air, for they neither sow nor reap nor gather into barns; yet your heavenly Father feeds them. Are you not of more value than they? Which of you by worrying can add one cubit to his stature?

"So why do you worry about clothing? Consider the lilies of the field, how they grow: they neither toil nor spin; and yet I say to you that even Solomon in all his glory was not arrayed like one of these. Now if God so clothes the grass of the field, which today is, and tomorrow is thrown into the oven, will He not much more clothe you, O you of little faith?

"Therefore do not worry, saying, 'What shall we eat?'

or 'What shall we drink?' or 'What shall we wear?' For after all these things the Gentiles seek. For your heavenly Father knows that you need all these things. But seek first the kingdom of God and His righteousness, and all these things shall be added to you. Therefore do not worry about tomorrow, for tomorrow will worry about its own things. Sufficient for the day is its own trouble" (Matthew 6:25-34).

Response: "O Lord my God, I will give thanks to You forever" (Psalm 30:12).

Take time to thank the Lord for His constant faithfulness.

Silence

Listen: "Show me Your ways, O Lord; teach me Your paths. Lead me in Your truth and teach me, for You are the God of my salvation; on You I wait all the day. Remember, O Lord, Your tender mercies and Your lovingkindnesses, for they have been from of old. Do not remember the sins of my youth, nor my transgressions; according to Your mercy remember me, for Your goodness' sake, O Lord. Good and upright is the Lord; therefore He teaches sinners in the way. The humble He guides in justice, and the humble He teaches His way" (Psalm 25:4-9).

Response: "Let the words of my mouth and the meditation of my heart, be acceptable in Your sight, O Lord, my strength and my Redeemer" (Psalm 19:14).

In silence, allow the Lord to help you picture yourself filled with His joy.

Intercession

Listen: "I was glad when they said to me, 'Let us go into the house of the Lord.' Our feet have been standing within your gates, O Jerusalem! Jerusalem is built as a city that is compact together, where the tribes go up, the tribes of the Lord, to the Testimony of Israel, to give thanks to the name of the Lord. For thrones are set there for judgment, the thrones of the house of David. Pray for peace of Jerusalem: 'May they prosper who love you. Peace be within your walls, prosperity within your palaces.' For the sake of my brethren and companions, I will now say, 'Peace be within you.' Because of the house of the Lord our God I will seek your good" (Psalm 122).

Response: Hear my prayers for my city.

Supplication

Listen: "I love the Lord, because He has heard my voice and my supplications" (Psalm 116:1).

Response: "Because He has inclined His ear to me, therefore I will call upon Him as long as I live" (Psalm 116:2).

Now turn over to the Lord the areas of your life in which you need to experience and express joy.

Guidance

Listen: "In all your ways acknowledge Him, and He shall direct your paths" (Proverbs 3:6).

Response: For this is God, my God forever and ever; He will be my guide (see Psalm 48:14).

Ask the Lord to guide you in all you do and say this day.

Commitment and Empowering

Listen: "For though He was crucified in weakness, yet He lives by the power of God. For we also are weak in Him, but we shall live with Him by the power of God toward you.

"Examine yourselves as to whether you are in the faith. Test yourselves. Do you not know yourselves, that Jesus Christ is in you?—unless indeed you are disqualified. But I trust that you will know that we are not disqualified.

"I pray to God that you do no evil, not that we should appear approved, but that you should do what is honorable, though we may seem disqualified. For we can do nothing against the truth, but for the truth. For we are glad when we are weak and you are strong. And this also we pray, that you may be made complete" (2 Corinthians 13:4-9).

Response: I will be of good comfort, of one mind, live in peace, and claim the God of love and He will be with me (see 2 Corinthians 13:11).

Joy is the sure sign that Christ lives in us. This is a day to live with joy!

Harvest House Books
by Lloyd John Ogilvie

CONVERSATION WITH GOD
Lloyd John Ogilvie shows you a fresh approach to prayer—one that is as much listening as speaking. He clearly and simply explains prayer's many dimensions and provides a 30-day guide so you can begin experiencing give-and-take conversation with God as part of your everyday life.

GOD'S BEST FOR MY LIFE
Better than your fondest hopes and expectations, God wants to give you His best for your life. This classic bestseller offers 365 devotions that invite you to discover, explore, and enjoy your loving Father each day.

PRAYING THROUGH THE TOUGH TIMES
The author gently guides you to pray for God's desires: confidence in His nearness; His grace to love others; and ability to see with His vision, grasping what the future can be when you put it in His hands.

QUIET MOMENTS WITH GOD
These daily prayers will help you nurture a special intimacy with God. You will experience God's blessed assurance as you are comforted by His boundless love and His promises to provide guidance and give strength.

THE RED EMBER IN THE WHITE ASH
Do you sometimes feel tired...burnt out...fearful to engage life? Dr. Ogilvie draws on Scripture to point you to the living and active Holy Spirit. As you see the darkness of fear and discouragement driven out by His flame of godly enthusiasm, you will experience hope and be able to love others with God's love.

To see sample chapters of these books, visit
www.harvesthousepublishers.com

HARVEST HOUSE
PUBLISHERS